RAISE YOUR RESILIENCE

YOU, YOUR FAMILY AND YOUR BUSINESS CAN ACHIEVE RESILIENCY IN AN UNCERTAIN WORLD

Kris Coleman
RED FIVE

gatekeeper press™
Columbus, Ohio

Raise Your Resilience: You, Your Family and Your Business Can Achieve Resiliency in an Uncertain World

Published by Gatekeeper Press
2167 Stringtown Rd, Suite 109
Columbus, OH 43123-2989
www.GatekeeperPress.com

The cover design, interior formatting, and typesetting for this book are entirely the product of the author. Gatekeeper Press did not participate in and is not responsible for any aspect of these elements.
ISBN (hardcover): 9781662904370
eISBN: 9781662904387

CONTENTS

INTRODUCTION

Do you need to survive the day? Yes. Does it bring new challenges? No doubt.

Do you want to thrive? Of course, you do.

But are you ready? Ready to take your life to a new level? Ready to face each challenge head-on? You should be. You can be.

The world is irrational, untiring, and unpredictable. If the recent COVID-19 pandemic holds any deeper meaning, it is a testament to that fact. Humans, secure at the top of nature's hierarchy, still fall victim to self-doubt, raw emotions, and desires. We, as a species, can be wonderful and yet, difficult. It's this imbalance of character, freewill, and fallibility that makes us – human. Miraculous. But how do we reconcile these incongruous parts of ourselves – and teach ourselves to reach beyond mere survival? How do we become our best selves, fulfilled? How do we truly thrive?

A key ingredient to fulfill that shared ambition to thrive is resiliency.

It's within reach. And it's within each of us. It's about knowing yourself – being self-reliant, prepared, ready. No matter where you began, what you look like, who you know, where you work, or what your dreams are – as an individual, equipped with freewill, you have the power to be resilient. In order to get there – you must get REAL™.

You must understand your reality and accept it. Find your weaknesses and address them. Acknowledge the unknown of the future and prepare for eventualities. Prepare for the Jackals.

The world is full of Jackals. Jackals are any kind of adversity, threat, or hazard that you might encounter as an individual, a family, a business. We will speak of the Jackal throughout this book, but know that it represents adversity – not a specific person.

I have used this Jackal approach in teaching around the world, in a respectful, informative, and visual manner. It doesn't reflect on culture, race, faith, or any facet of life. The learner puts the Jackal into context for themselves. You know your own Jackals.

Resiliency is based on the individual, and their ability to deal with the Jackals.

You are the cornerstone to your own resilience. And if families have resilient heads of households; and businesses have resilient founders and leaders – those entities too, will be resilient. It starts with the person. It starts with you.

Navigating this world requires REAL Awareness, Mindset, Fitness, Skills, and Relationships.

Source: Red Five

Resiliency goes beyond oneself. You must also ready your family for the real impacts of the economy, politics and environment. Prepare your business, so it can properly support you and your family for the long-term. Your livelihood must be attuned to the real threats that may exist and you must understand your vulnerabilities to proactively manage those risks.

We have all experienced adversity – tragedy, family illness, loss of friendship, death of a brother on the battlefield, termination of employment, violence, prejudice, retirement, scandal, heartbreak. Adversity, which quickly leads to feelings of disappointment that fosters anxiety and doubt, is unavoidable in life. Some Jackals you can expect, such as the death of a family member. These real-life experiences can often take a toll physically, mentally, and emotionally. It's similar for businesses – filing for bankruptcy, losing a large client, an acquisition or takeover, supply chain disruption, violence in the workplace, or the loss of a founder.

Since the dawn of existence, we humans have experienced a near perfect arch of the curveball that life hurls at us – loss and wins, suffering and joy, tears and laughter, rejection and acceptance, doubt and confidence. As the science of evolution has proven, life on our planet requires the ability to adapt, recover, grow, and ultimately, persevere. Some Jackals are man-made. Sometimes we do it to ourselves. Sometimes other Jackals are intentional.

September 11, 2001 is a date that will forever be remembered in our history books. Families of 2,977 human beings lost loved ones. The impact of 9-11 didn't stop when the dust finally settled at ground-zero in the subsequent years. The event sent shock waves across our country that shook communities, businesses, families, and individuals to their very core. But through the extreme adversity and pain we have mourned, survived and learned. Based on the handling of the stressful and emotional experiences we endured, we have all emerged more resilient – even if this transformation has happened unconsciously.

We navigated the way back from the brink. We leveraged emotional and physical tools to recover and rebuild. We tapped into our character, our grit – strength we may not have known we had.

And over time, the pieces of ourselves that were broken from tremendous tragedy have been put back together with even more strength. Through this process of experience, assessment, acceptance, decision-making, re-energizing and rebuilding, we grow. This process is the path to resilience. But can frequently re-define the individual.

If you want to thrive, you need resiliency in three areas; yourself, your family and your business. And you need to get there smartly and quickly in this uncertain world. The Jackals are everywhere and they may be specific to you. You just have to be ready.

You have a need. We have the answer. It's time to get REAL.

WHAT IS RESILIENCY?

Various entities provide definitions for resiliency. In general, it is defined as the ability to bounce back from adversity; the capacity to recover quickly from difficulties; or, the capability to adjust easily to misfortune or change.

People have it, organizations have it. We have all heard people say, "she's tough as nails" or "he's strong as an ox." And we're familiar with phrases attributed to a city that has experienced a tragedy, such as, "El Paso Strong" or "Boston Strong." Resilience is characterized, sometimes incorrectly, as strength's equal. It's important to recognize the difference between physical and emotional strength vs. physical and emotional resilience. In truth, resilience is related to strength, but more like an older and wiser sibling. Resilience embodies a higher level of understanding, growth, and experience.

Jackals can be man-made, natural disasters, bad business deals, bad people or just bad timing with no preparation. What Jackals have you prepared for?

Is your business facing Jackals at the door everyday as you try to maintain cash flow? Are your investors nipping at your heels because you cannot lead your business during this pandemic?

For some cities and countries – the Jackals might be the weather, Mother Nature, or crime and terrorism. New York rebounded from crime in the 1980s, and 9-11 in 2001. Joplin, Missouri rebounded after the tornado of 2011. The Summer of 2019 was waterlogged; all along the Arkansas River including my home town of Fort Smith. The town has bounced back and the river keeps flowing. The Pentagon and the Washington, DC area rebounded from 9/11, while many cities along the Gulf and Atlantic coasts have suffered from hurricanes.

The San Francisco Bay area has been resilient in the face of adversity over the years. Yes, they have had their share of protests, active shooters, and crime, but they are known for their recovery after major earthquakes. On April 18, 1906 they endured the Great San Francisco Earthquake that is estimated to have been near an 8.0 on the Richter Scale. An estimated 3,000 people were killed as fires broke out across the city and raged for three days. Almost 30,000 buildings were destroyed and numerous businesses and families were without shelter and services. The city by the Bay bounced back.

Again in 1989, San Francisco was hit by the 6.9 Loma Prieta earthquake. This quake struck during an historic World Series between the Oakland Athletics and the San Francisco Giants. This quake killed 67 people and wrought $5 billion in damages. While Candlestick Park, where the game was to be played, was relatively safe, many parts of San Francisco saw extensive damage. They learned from this tragic incident, employing new construction code and mitigation efforts, initiating recovery planning and emergency funding sources, and creating new legislation.

Many of these resiliency aspects came into play in 2019 when wildfires again ravaged 260,000 acres in California – destroying thousands of homes and businesses, wrecking the school year, and taking five victims from their families. Tens of thousands had to evacuate and millions faced blackouts.

New York was strong after 9-11. Boston was strong after the Marathon Bombing. But in the wake of those events, the communities and the families that make up those cities displayed a different kind of strength. A kind of strength that can't fit on a bumper sticker. They had endured real pain. They lost loved ones. They lost breadwinners. But they bounced back and buoyed their communities, which made Boston, New York, El Paso, Houston, and New Orleans even stronger.

I was privileged to live in Norway for two years working within their culture, their society, and experiencing the global festival of the Winter Olympics. I grew to love the Norwegian people, understanding their language and culture, and embracing things the way they do. They are a tough people, with a long history, Viking culture, and a love of nature. During World War II they formed a successful resistance against the Germans and carried out numerous missions to thwart the advance of fascism in their country and in Scandinavia writ large. They resisted the scourge of Nazi occupation and established connections with the Allies.

Not only did the Norwegian people demonstrate their resilience during occupation, but they demonstrate it every day and make it part of their lives. One of the things I loved about my time there was the experience of nature and weather. The darkness and cold of the long winter, contrasted with the very long sunny days of summer. What the Norwegians taught me was that there is no such thing as bad weather, just bad clothing. So, as all good operators know today – the Norwegians have known forever – wear the right clothing for the weather you have. You can get through bad weather with the right gear and the right mindset.

Is your family ready for the natural disaster Jackals in your region?

Resilience is something that goes with the person, is brought along by the family, and is inherent in the business once established. It is not something that sits in the corner like a rifle or a medical kit. It is not an inanimate object whose traits bestow upon the possessor the ability to persevere. No, resilience goes with you when you travel, either as an individual on vacation or as a professional on a business trip. It's not enough to be "resilient" at home; you need to develop these traits and carry them with you as you would your wallet, your keys, as part of your "Everyday Carry." Whatever you would normally bring along for your day's excursion – resilience should be part of that toolkit.

When you travel, note that you are entering a new space that has different threats and hazards, and the Jackals you had experienced in and around your home have changed now that you have landed in a new environment. Don't bring along your local perceptions of safety into your new environment. There may be significantly less law enforcement in your destination city; or perhaps there are challenges completely different due to culture, health issues, government (or lack of), or civil unrest.

Question your standard for risk and preparedness, and understand that in that new location things are now different. Make it a conscious thought.

Resiliency is a state of mind. It is a learned skill and it is a critical ingredient to surviving in the world today.

Resiliency is a national security imperative. Resiliency will see our communities through natural disasters, and help us as we support others who are in need.

As Americans, we have inherited a proud legacy forged by resiliency. Our forefathers bore great responsibility and hardship in carving out a worthy future for our country, and by their example, we endeavor to carry on that tradition and pioneering spirit. Many of us have ancestors who may have sought their fortunes across the Atlantic all the way to the Great Plains and the formidable Rocky Mountains. They may have lived through the Great Depression or the Dustbowl. Every generation meets its challenges and foes – it is left to the character, wisdom and resiliency of our leaders and our neighbors that shape the outcome.

Once we accept the fact that resiliency is mission-critical and a human imperative for individuals, families, communities, businesses, and our country, it's important that we measure it.

WHERE DO YOU FIND RESILIENCY?

Historically, the challenge has been how to measure resilience. You might even be wondering, "can you measure resilience?" It's a valid question. For such an intangible characteristic, it's hard to nail down.

Some have measured resilience by calculating impact (think, end results) by asking, "Did you come out of the situation ok? Are you better than before? Or did it consume your being, your life, your company, to the point of irreparable emotional, financial, or physical impact?"

In many cases it's difficult to measure because it requires a tragedy or incident to actually determine if what was thought to be resilience, actually plays out as a strength in the aftermath. Or were the actions just theoretical? Was the individual's ego and character not actually put to the test? Was it simply a "plan on a shelf" that resulted in a less than desirable outcome?

The results of resiliency are all around us. They are easy to find if you know where to look. Individuals who have conquered cancer; companies bouncing back from bankruptcy; wounded warriors re-entering society; family members redefining their lives after a setback. These are a handful of scenarios that yield substantial and real resiliency results.

We can test the ability of people and companies to be resilient. We can create a scale, ask specific questions, and measure the results of the answers to apply a score to those results.

There are currently several examples of scales that all standardize the method of measuring resilience. Any of them will work. What's important to accept and understand is that resilience is, indeed, measurable and applicable to humans and, therefore, a teachable or trainable characteristic.

In the end, resiliency is achievable by people, and by transfer, families and communities can become resilient. Furthermore, companies, that consist of people, can be characterized as resilient. Therefore it is also possible to **create a system** around which resilience is built. **Resilience that is systematized. Now, we can now measure it; we can adjust it; we can teach it (and pass it on).**

Resilience has been important through the ages because it has allowed animals and mankind to develop, adapt and improve, thereby strengthening the species for survival. Some may characterize resiliency as a naturally occurring trait, but the reality is that resiliency is the culmination of learned behaviors and attributes. Each one of us, no matter our physical appearance, health history or perceived intellect, can learn to have our own Resilience System.

The REAL System for tracking resiliency

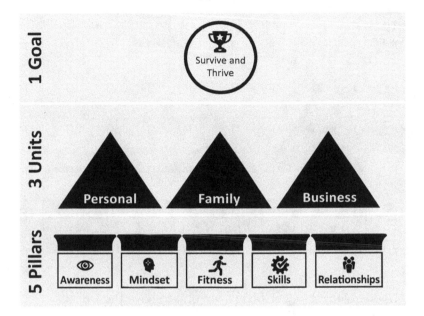

We assert the system that works begins with the end in mind – the 1 goal, to survive and thrive. The 3 units that facilitate and enable us to achieve the 1 goal are – personal, family, and business (your livelihood). And, in order to achieve resilience each of those units must exercise the 5 pillars – awareness, mindset, fitness, skills and relationships. This is the REAL 5-3-1 System for resilience.

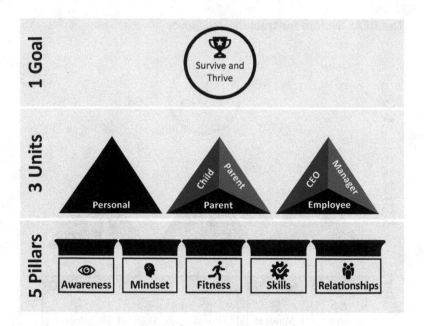

*Need at least one person in each unit to have the 5 pillars

1 Goal

In today's world I have found there is one goal in mind when seeking resilience. The **1 Goal is to individually survive and thrive regardless of whatever life throws at you**. That's it. Simple, huh? How hard can it be? Let's dig a little deeper.

As Simon Sinek says in his famous TED Talk, let's "start with why"… why do we do anything? Why does a company exist? Why would someone buy your product? Why would you follow a system that improves your life and your family's future? We want our tribe to be happy, be safe, be healthy, be prosperous. *To survive and thrive – that's why. It's that simple.*

3 Units

It's probably safe to say we all have experienced obstacles and sometimes harsh lessons life throws at us, especially when we aren't looking, or aren't prepared. These trials test us in different ways and impact different aspects of our lives, including our personal self, our family, or our business.

Within the REAL System, there are **three units through which we must apply resilience. They include – personal resilience, family readiness, and business preparedness.** We will cover them in detail, as we move through this book.

Personal Resilience is Unit One

It all starts with the individual unit. If the individual unit is strong and resilient, then we can build on that foundation for the other two. Some elements are found already ingrained in us as a result of inherited traits and family upbringing. We can add to this with new personal skills that are achievable and sustainable over time.

Family Readiness is Unit Two

The family must apply their individual resilience as a unit and build upon it so the family has a sense of readiness for whatever they encounter. It could be the result of a tornado, difficult economic times, a divorce, a move cross-country or around the globe, or a prolonged illness.

Business Preparedness is Unit Three

Lastly, the livelihood for the family unit must be prepared. Business preparedness applies to all aspects of the organization – if only some of the employees are resilient, and only some small units within the business are ready – is the business truly prepared? We will talk about how the business is resilient because it is prepared to weather and navigate anything the world can throw at it, including decline in revenue, legal challenges, bankruptcy, globalization, or shifting competition and demand.

Still with me? Just checking.

5 Pillars

There are five pillars of resilience. They are:

👁 REAL Awareness

You have a firm grasp on reality and make decisions based on current and accurate information and intelligence. Your personal, family, and business awareness must be heightened. Your awareness of yourself, others and outliers must be consistent and attuned to the risks and opportunities that exist.

🧠 REAL Mindset

You can achieve a mindset that will support you in winning, surviving and finding a way through. Don't give up. The right mindset is critical. It is an enthusiastic way of looking at grit and what it takes to get through the obstacles ahead. Never give up.

🏃 REAL Fitness

Your physical and emotional fitness are key to your ability to bounce back. Stress and emotional instability can create distractions, reduce elasticity in your life, and make it harder to deal with the ups and downs that we all endure.

⚙ REAL Skills

Your skills are core to the physical and mental attributes and learned skills that we need to survive and thrive. At the most basic level, it is how to find food, water, shelter, and defend yourself. At a deeper, more sophisticated level, it is how to plan, how to recognize threats, how to adjust our plans and move smartly to new objectives. How to negotiate and navigate amongst our friends, allies and enemies – in your personal life, as well as the business world.

👥 REAL Relationships

Know your trusted circle – your family, your spouse, your neighbors, and your community. You need them to survive and you must nurture them to thrive. Regardless of your race, color or geography – each of us has, and must deal with, relationships. Learn your personal best, accept others and yourself to make the most of it all.

We'll explore each of these in coming chapters, but know that they form the five pillars upon which the three units can launch you into the stratosphere of success you desire.

REAL 5-3-1 forms the foundation to build your best life. It all starts with resiliency. Now is the time to build a life that will bounce back from adversity; that will recover when thrown off balance; that will allow you and your family to thrive.

If you take care of the three units, and ensure your five pillars are strong, your system of resilience will run efficiently.

If you put the system into action, your family's lifestyle, your business and livelihood will be enhanced and driven. And you will be closer to achieving your one goal.

WHY? THE 1 GOAL, THAT'S WHY

Today we live in a convoluted, complex ecosystem of varying demands, stressors, peer pressures, familial strains, and technological stimuli. Two generations ago, we did not have this huge volume of inputs to address – job and family were the driving stress points for those growing up in the early 20th century. Now, we find ourselves tethered to our digital lifelines – our smartphones, laptops, WiFi, apps. We are inundated with technology, password requirements, texts, digital profiles, likes, and swiping right. Sound familiar?

We need technology to achieve the 1 Goal. We need it to survive and thrive – that is what life is about. So technology cannot be ignored, and it cannot be diminished – it needs to be managed and optimized.

We live in a time where we can virtually control our lives from the palm of our hands. It's no wonder how easy it is to forget to look up and recognize the real external forces that form our environment.

COVID-19 and civil unrest have highlighted the need for resilience. The global pandemic has been a complicating factor in the recent civil unrest in the U.S. racial conflict has been an unresolved issue, and instances of police interaction, excessive force or brutality have added to the conflict. As the protests grow, so do the interactions among throngs of people complicating the need for social distancing and other health issues. As we have seen over the past few months, civil unrest has become more common and has not been limited to the major cities, but has also spread to some smaller cities where protests, both peaceful and violent, have developed.

Resilience in uneasy times and during times of conflict is crucial. It is important to have it and use it personally, with your family and in your livelihood or business. During these times of civil unrest, were you prepared when the protests approached your neighborhood or in your business district? How did you adjust your operations? What did your family do differently?

The urban world that many of us live in today, is a numbing, emasculating environment that has altered our natural tendencies. The urban rhythm of life reduces us to staring at screens, engaging from behind closed doors – but something vital is missing from this existence. We are meant to live fully – engaging with each other, getting our hands dirty, and experiencing the world around us.

It is time to get REAL and step out of the skewed and digitally enhanced shadows in which you've been hiding. It's time to reset and get back to reality. Now more than ever, our communities, our country, and our world need a dose of reality. We need to get back to the basics of humanity. We can use the REAL 5-3-1 System to get there.

The Great Disruptors

Technology

New technology tells two compelling narratives. At once, it's transformative powers can increase our quality of life, but on the other hand it can breakdown the authenticity of being REAL. People are not present in real world relationships If they are spending too much time on their devices. Technological innovation brings great strides in business, healthcare breakthroughs, energy efficiency and individual autonomy; but the tools that come with it can be used to harm our civility and make it easier for the Jackals.

Social Media Pressures

Time Magazine stated that today, 92 percent of all American 2-year-olds have an online presence. Parents, as early adopters and prolific posters of personal information, have made social media and the relinquishment of our privacy a common thing.

Children and teens experience additional pressures to overshare things that were once private at that age. Photographs, locations, and life events that used to be highly meaningful and private are now seen as "must shares" and in not sharing, some children feel shame and embarrassment.

Children today are undertaking the grueling process of growing up online – through a filtered prism of reality that allows them to hide the ugly and painful parts of coming of age. Online personas – a contradiction of terms – is an accepted reality and we "teach" children the strategy of enhancing this altered version of themselves. Real stress and crisis of identity simply comes with the territory of "growing up online" today.

Threats to Privacy

Online presence and the oversharing of personal information is one area of privacy that needs to be addressed. Young people are feeling the pressure to share, and are not giving that post or that Instagram photo a second thought even though it might have a long term effect. It could hurt their reputation, their personal brand or their relationships with real people.

The vast online world that children grow up in and adults navigate every day is a massive target. In the industry, cyber experts talk about the "attack surface," which is the different parts of the system that are available to the Jackals to attack. In the online world today – there are a myriad of attack surfaces, all exposing the vulnerabilities of the human user, and the weaknesses inherent in the sharing systems.

It requires a concerted effort for people to shield their privacy through education, diligence, technological awareness, and good practices. Individuals and parents have to keep up with the technology trends, as well as the adversarial tactics that seek to compromise their privacy.

Alternative to Reality

From the start, they must be aware of and protect their identities in a relentless technological wilderness. By the time they are in their teens and contending with social acceptance, peer pressure and body image (to name a few), they are already spending more energy on playing defense than on focusing on healthy personal development. Young people today are balancing much more than just homework, piano recitals, and football practice. They have an alternate universe they carry in their pockets that drains every last drop of time and energy in their day. And this is accepted as normal. As noted by Scientific American, the brain is the organ in the body that expends the most energy – if that organ is spending the majority of its energy protecting itself, what is left for individual play, creativity, and social development?

Humans of all ages need to get outdoors, innovate, create, imagine and play. This helps them discern between virtual worlds and the real one. This gives them a huge advantage as they develop and it's something we do less and less as we get older. Children are far better learners than the most sophisticated computers applying artificial intelligence. According to Alison Gopnik, American professor of psychology and affiliate professor of philosophy at the University of California, Berkeley, "kids are out in the real world," and not inside a computer. They are interacting with others. "They're curious." They are active learners.

Resilience requires having a realistic view of the conditions we face. We cannot be resilient if our standard is a fantasy or artificial. As humans that stare at screens all day, whether in an office cubicle, a laptop at home or a tablet/smart phone on the go – we need to embrace continuous learning, preferably outdoor learning, to achieve, and maintain our sense of reality and increase our resilience.

If we stay inside working on our digital profiles and streaming entertainment, we are not likely to gain the constructive biofeedback we could have had by skinning a knee skateboarding, bruising a knuckle working on a car, or getting a little sunshine from being outside on a hike. Those are all REAL feelings. On the other hand, being verbally abused (or abusing another) in a social media post, getting into a "fight" in a text thread, or staring at shopping websites most of the day does not promote one's reality either. We need an effective ability to interact with other humans in a face-to-face manner. This is the core to our ability to bounce back to the challenges of REAL life. REAL life calls for REAL resilience.

As stated before, not all technology is bad. It helps us stay connected to family over great distances, allows us to interact with friends that we have lost contact with, and see grandkids that we wouldn't be able to otherwise. BUT, it's all about how we as humans CHOOSE to use it. It shouldn't be about how the technology pulls us in and consumes our lives. That path leads to passive living, weakness, and a reduced ability to deal with adversity when it lands squarely in our lap.

The modern life we live is full of stressors. Technology can exacerbate them, as can social media, and those elements that we internalize. And when we don't handle stress well, it can lead to further complications with our family, our personal relationships, our spousal intimacy and the most studied topic – our health.

According to the Holmes and Rahe Stress Scale, the top ten stressful life events that can adversely affect our health are:

1. Death of a spouse
2. Divorce
3. Marriage separation

16

4. Imprisonment
5. Death of a close family member
6. Injury or illness
7. Marriage
8. Job loss
9. Marriage reconciliation
10. Retirement

Any one of these would bring with it significant stress. Are you ready to deal with any of the above? Some awful combination of the above? It's not about who is at fault, or how you may have been treated unfairly – stop redirecting the blame and trying to find fault. Own the situation and be better prepared. It won't stop the grief; it won't reduce the pain; but being better prepared can reduce the duration of the challenge and perhaps keep it from snowballing into something worse than it has to be.

In the context of the 1 Goal – people need to be able to better cope with stress, adversity, and challenges. It's like armor against the Jackals; it improves our constitution, our ability to endure.

COVID-19 is wreaking havoc with the above list, bringing multiple combinations into our homes and businesses. And when we have these Jackals arriving on our doorstep each day it can have a debilitating effect on our health. Use the REAL 5-3-1 System.

Don't let the Jackals start the ball rolling downhill. Get REAL now, with the 5-3-1 System to achieve the 1 Goal. Keep the Jackals at bay, manage the stress ahead of time.

4

CONDITIONS THAT AFFECT RESILIENCY

Some individuals handle setbacks well, some don't. We know we must face challenges and handle the consequences of those outcomes. Life goes on – and so must we. For some, life will never be the same as it was before the incident. For others, the life ahead will be like it was before – as if it never happened. Why do some people and businesses bounce back better than others? Is it cultural? Is it process? Is it luck? Is it learned?

Can you, as an individual, be more resilient? We know you can. But, it's a choice. Choose to be resilient.

Young adults and teenagers are in many cases coming into their adulthood with less ability to deal with reality. They haven't had to change a flat tire (and certainly not at night in the rain). They haven't spent an overnight in the outdoors in the woods. This isn't a condition that only affects adults in the city. Conversely, people growing up in rural areas don't know what it is like to navigate the concrete jungle of the city, such as during rush hour or going from dinner to clubbing. Each of those experiences provides some learning, but if everyone is staring at a screen, the learning isn't happening. Children and young adults fare better when they get outside and get active. They are particularly more resilient to stress and adversity when they experience nature, according to a study by Nancy M. Wells, PhD, Cornell University.

It is important to our evolution as a society and our country that our younger generations do not turn into screen zombies, unable to deal with adversity and life's challenges.

Our military and our first responder agencies do a great job of preparing their people for the challenges of the real world. Boot camps and training academies immerse candidates in artificially dangerous and stressful environments, giving them a chance to experience significant failures, and giving them the tools to bounce back from those experiences in a constructive learning environment.

The COVID-19 pandemic has highlighted some aspects of resilience, specifically how preparation can have unintended but highly impactful effects on your resilience. Back in the early 2000's a friend had a heart attack. He was the poster child for health. A runner, with healthy weight, clean eating, and regular checkups, showed no indication of a cardiac issue. But there he was, suffering from a heart attack due to genetics and stress. So, while he had done all he could to avoid a health issue, to be proactively healthy to avoid a heart attack – it was interesting to know that all he had done to avoid a heart attack had actually become crucially important to his *recovery* . . . his resilience. Realize that some of the things that you are doing with all the best intentions may not stop the "bad thing" from happening that you initially intended to avoid. BUT, your efforts may provide you with other benefits that are not obvious to you when the bad thing occurs.

We are seeing some of those same instances during COVID-19. We can all wear a mask, wash our hands, socially distance, decontaminate our deliveries, and hand sanitize. But in the end, with a virus this contagious – anyone seems to be likely to contract the disease. Some people experience no symptoms, others have more serious complications and even death. So, while we cannot control the virus per se, we can control how healthy we can be as individuals. And being healthy will have its benefits – whether for COVID-19, the flu or the unexpected cardiac event on the horizon. Health and fitness – emotionally and physically – play a key role in our resilience.

In personal, family, and business preparedness it's critical to apply these concepts. In case of work disruptions, is your business setup with the ability to work remotely? Do you have business continuity plans? How about action plans for emergencies?

Personally, are you ready with cash savings? Can you take the opportunity now, during COVID-19 to get training to enhance your career? What can make you healthier personally and professionally?

And for those business owners, what about a succession plan for your leadership? Are you ready to hand off the reins to the next in line? Do you have someone identified? Are they properly prepared to manage the company, steer it through tough times, and align the resources with strategy?

During the Tsunami of 2004, on December 26 a magnitude 9.0 quake in the Indian Ocean unleashed the power of 23,000 Hiroshima bombs, according to the U.S. Geological Survey. That energy was transferred into the nearby ocean creating waves that were moving at the speed of a jet aircraft. The result was more than 150,000 dead or missing with millions of people left homeless across 11 countries. It has been recorded as the deadliest tsunami in modern history.

In Sri Lanka, some of the lessons learned included the importance of trees near the shoreline. Mature trees provided a brake for the waves as they crashed into the shore, but before they hit businesses and moved further inland. Many crops and gardens were protected and now new coconut trees are being added that double as crops themselves. The importance of diversification of livelihoods and businesses became clear as so many companies and families experienced catastrophic losses.

Interviews and investigations have shown that people who had greater awareness of the signs of a tsunami immediately fled to higher ground and went away from the curiously receding shoreline. Animals seemed to sense the danger and knew to flee. Very few animal corpses were found in the aftermath. Are you aware of the dangers in the city where you live? What are the signs that a tsunami is coming? What about a tornado from a dangerous thunderstorm in the plains? Are you ready for a wildfire scenario as it approaches your home or business?

Employers know that veterans and first responders are almost always strong performers during employment screening, scenario-based interviews and discussions that require them to think on their feet and solve problems in their head. The reasons for their success is what they have been through in the real world. Quick thinking and decision-making in life and death situations based on training and experience forged their resilience in real time in the real world.

They have traveled, they have experienced heartbreak and homesickness, they have endured personal loss and fear, and they have worked and celebrated as a team. They have dealt with a diverse spectrum of other human beings from all walks of life, and experienced empathy and tears together. They have had to deal with challenging communications, different cultural norms, opposing views on religion and family, and challenging climatic elements. And they have been to the edge and had to stare their enemy, and death, in the eye, as others try to do them harm. Those environments and experiences change people forever.

Some people ask themselves, "how do I achieve those experiences or how do I get the 'eye of the tiger' to achieve warrior status, or become the stoic samurai." We all want the 1 Goal – to survive and thrive.

Regardless of the conditions in which you find yourself, the geography in which you live, or the level of affluence you have, you can now achieve the grit required to succeed in this world of confusion and chaos. Back to the REAL 5-3-1 System.

THE 5 PILLARS OF RESILIENCY

Resilience is comprised of actions, behaviors, and thoughts that can be learned and developed in anyone.

A combination of factors contribute to resilience. Many studies show that the primary factor in resilience is having caring and supportive relationships within and outside the family. Relationships that are based on love and trust, provide role models and offer encouragement and reassurance, help bolster a person's resilience. This brings us back to engaging in the human experience, talking to people, getting out of the house and interacting with others in a way that expands our data set for learning, communicating, and decision-making.

> **"**
> Resilience can be learned. The capabilities that underlie resilience can be strengthened at any age. The brain and other biological systems are most adaptable early in life. Yet while their development lays the foundation for a wide range of resilient behaviors, it is never too late to build resilience. Age-appropriate, health-promoting activities can significantly improve the odds that an individual will recover from stress-inducing experiences. For example, regular **"**

> **"** physical exercise, stress-reduction practices, and programs that actively build executive function and self-regulation skills can improve the abilities of children and adults to cope with, adapt to, and even prevent adversity in their lives. Adults who strengthen these skills in themselves can better model healthy behaviors for their children, thereby improving the resilience of the next generation.
> – Harvard University's Center on the Developing Child **"**

Five pillars applied to the three units = the one goal.

This is the system. This gets you there. Commit to the five pillars, apply them across the three units and you will arrive at the one goal.

Use the system, support your three units with the five pillars.

There are five PILLARS that make up REAL resilience:

REAL Awareness, REAL Mindset, REAL Fitness, REAL Skills, and REAL Relationships are the five pillars to achieving REAL resilience. Those concepts are bolstered by other factors and are a means to achieving a resilient lifestyle.

These five also apply to each of the three units – personal resiliency, family readiness, and business preparedness. Applying them smartly within each, puts you well on the way to a high level of strength and resiliency in your life.

👁 REAL Awareness

Awareness is defined by Merriam-Webster as, "knowledge and understanding that something is happening or exists." In the context of your REAL-ity and resilience, REAL Awareness is the ability to notice, put in context, and realistically digest what is going on around you. That includes the physical, as well as your current emotional and psychological state. If you don't have awareness of yourself, it is impossible to accurately understand the reality around you and how it relates to the decisions, plans and actions you must take. It affects how you can successfully react to actions being taken against you, or developments that are not in your best personal or business interests.

24

🧠 REAL Mindset

A REAL mindset is everything. It's how you put all the various aspects of your life together and it's the playbook for how you move through your day, your week, your life. Having a survival mindset is key for military and law enforcement personnel, as they move through their careers. A REAL mindset is absolutely crucial to living your best life, helping your family achieve the most and getting your business and livelihood to the pinnacle.

> How you think about the world you live in makes a big difference to the way you will react to it. Thinking negatively and regularly using the words "I can't," "never will," and comparing yourself to others are all indicators of thinking traps. For example, Johnny is a great basketball player. He is great therefore I cannot be as good as he is. I can't make the team because I'm not great. While the first statement may be true, the others create a thinking trap that you can't make the basketball team. Why not change your thinking from the beginning? Johnny is a great basketball player. I can be as good or better than he is. I will make the basketball team this year. While it appears to be a subtle change of words, it is all it takes to shift the many psychological factors that come into play. In the end, it is a personal choice as to how you want to think about life. Use your power of choice wisely because when an individual can change their thinking to a more positive mindset, it is empowering and liberating.

A REAL mindset allows you to separate the noise from what's important, it allows you to clearly see what needs to be done to achieve your goals. It allows you to constructively ignore those that are trying to compete for your attention, leading you to poor decisions, incomplete information, or biased outcomes.

❝
"If you are not the calm, then you are the chaos."
– Jeff Banman, Founder of MindsetRadio
❞

REAL Fitness

Fitness has long been understood as playing a critical role in how individuals respond to stressors. Fitness is a key determinant of success in the military, first responders, law enforcement, park rangers, medical professionals, business leaders, and parents. Stress has a direct impact on our physiological self. The greater our individual ability to process stress and reduce it through fitness, the more we will experience enhanced performance, decision-making, improved cognitive processes and personal empathy. We need to be physically and emotionally fit, combining physical fitness, wellness, and emotional stability is the path to REAL Fitness.

According to the Mayo Clinic, fitness and exercise act as stress busters. Fitness allows an individual to better process the cortisol producing anxiety that consumes many of us today. It produces endorphins that help us feel better, relax and improves our mood. Exercise is a form of meditation in that getting your mind into "the zone" takes your mind off the stressful activities of the day and allows us to regenerate, energize and increase blood flow to all parts of the body. Find an activity that you enjoy and get outside for some fresh air. It will help your resilience. While you work on your fitness with others, you can increase your social skills as well.

Well-being and emotional stability must be achieved for optimal resilience. Meditation (whether in a dark and calming room or on a long-distance motorcycle ride) is when your mind is free of distraction and can be allowed to rest, recover, and create or change its focus away from the daily grind. If chaos is the driver of your daily routine, it will be hard to separate the noisy distractions from what could be the warning bells that you need to hear clearly.

REAL Skills
Skills are learnable. Skills are attainable through advice, perfect practice, and repetition. REAL skills are those

particular abilities that are directly applicable to resilience, survival, practicality, planning, communications, and maneuvering through life. REAL skills include self-defense, finding and sustaining key elements of survival (food, water, shelter, purpose), and employing certain tools in specific circumstances. REAL skills include starting a fire (without a lighter); changing a tire (without calling AAA); defending yourself when threatened; sourcing food and water; and moving through your world safely, whether in a car or on foot. Planning in a professional and deliberate fashion for your family's resilience is key to your readiness. Being the best, most responsible business leader, so that you and your employees are prepared and can thrive.

REAL Relationships

REAL relationships are healthy, productive, challenging interactions with people intent on helping you grow, helping your family prosper, and helping your business expand and stay lean and profitable.

You and your spouse or significant other need a REAL relationship – one based on trust, honesty, reality, and a healthy emotional and physical existence. Your children and parents offer another level of stability, reasonableness for bouncing ideas around, and a safe place to talk about the future, exciting ideas, dreams, and goals.

Reaching out to other human beings provides individuals with support, different perspectives on situations and options, and creates an emotional bond with others that produces optimism and hope.

REAL relationships in the physical world that require face to face human interaction are critical to a person's ability to be resilient. Clearly, this factor depends on the quality and mindset of those with whom we connect; and therefore, the relationships must meet a standard. Connecting with negative people, poor role models, and pessimists does not promote positive relationships. However, connecting with family members, meeting with friends, interacting with and talking to colleagues does help broaden your information set.

Religious groups, neighborhoods, peer groups and communities also offer tremendous advantage, and positivity in their relationships. They allow for the creation of REAL positive energy and enthusiasm; personal connections and friendships; and a support structure for when unexpected adversity arrives at your doorstep.

The 5 Pillars can help you with your Jackals. Use the pillars to prepare for them. Use the pillars to fight them off.

Other factors

According to the American Psychological Association (APA) there are several additional factors that are associated with resilience, including:

- [ ] The capacity to make realistic plans and take steps to carry them out.
- [ ] Skills in communication and problem solving.
- [ ] A positive view of yourself and confidence in your strengths and abilities.
- [ ] The capacity to manage strong feelings and impulses.

Planning is a key element to our approach. It's not enough to wake up and make up your mind. As difficult as that is – there is so much more to take into account. One must be sophisticated enough to take it all in, make smart decisions, plan, and adjust. Act . . . and then observe, make adjustments again. All moving to the same ultimate goal by supporting the pillars and informing the units.

Communication skills are critical in any relationship and any business. We can always improve communications and we have to pick the right channel and timing for the message, as well as the audience. Just like this book – it's to the point to match the attention span of today's readers.

Emotional intelligence to address one's self confidence and self-worth is absolutely necessary. If you don't figure out how to accept and love yourself first, others will not follow. Take stock of what and who you are – accept it, embrace it. You have to learn to manage anger, jealousy, frustration, love and lust, and understand what they are and how to manage them. Emotions can cloud your judgment, and as we talk about later – they can skew your reality, leading to incorrect decisions and undesired outcomes.

All of these items have a common thread in that they are dealing with REAL world experiences, real people, real issues. They require an optimistic perspective and an ability to critically and consciously think about the topics in the present.

The 5 Pillars of resilience provide the support needed for people to become resilient. They may or may not be inherent in people, but they can be learned, and they can be improved upon.

6

THE 3 UNITS OF RESILIENCY

We have now articulated the five pillars and various other factors that create the foundation for resilience, whether it be a person, a family, or a business. Next, we will look closely at the three units. Each of the five pillars can be applied within each unit. Awareness, Mindset, Fitness, Skills, Relationships.

Across the pillars and units there are interdependencies. There are overlaps. The units and the pillars aren't perfectly clean compartments with defined borders and inventories. In fact, we embrace those overlaps across the units as strengthening and self-reinforcing ties among and between the different units. The overlay of the five pillars across the units is a resilient trait in and of itself. Don't try to fix it – it isn't a problem; and it's not wasteful – it's purposeful.

Personal Resilience

REAL Awareness – In your daily routine you should wake up and be aware of where you are. What house you are in. What city. What relationship. What is your reality? REAL-ity. What's up with your family, your spouse, your job? What are the state of affairs in your neighborhood? Your spiritual status. Mental health. What are things like in and around your life – who are the influencers? Are they providing you positive energy or draining away your life force? **Know what is important, what is not. You need self-awareness for you and the other 4 REAL pillars.**

REAL Mindset – Every day you wake up, you should be prepared for a positive day. You should be prepared to make the right choices. You can make the right choices. The power of choice is extremely important and powerful. Use your power of choice wisely because as we know, a bad choice today can lead to an undesired outcome year from now (especially true on the internet). **Great choices that you make this morning can lead to an outstandingly successful afternoon. What you believe, is what comes around.**

REAL Fitness – Everyone has their means of staying emotionally and physically fit. Are you where you want to be? What do you need to do to get there? Who can help you? If you have arrived at your fitness goal, **whether you are as emotionally and physically fit as you want to be – ask yourself, what are you going to do today to sustain that fitness? Well-being, meditation, physical activity – get outside, free your mind.**

REAL Skills – Skills, if you don't have them – let's get them. We need shelter, food, water, self-defense as a starting point. We need to deal with the pervasive technology and privacy issues, as well as first aid and health issues. Start with the basics, we aren't trying to turn everyone into commandos or SWAT team members. We are trying to build a foundation, and add to that in a reasonable fashion. Moving the needle, reasonably, within budget and with a purpose of reaching a level of skill that makes sense for you personally. We then can address the need for the ability to plan, collect information, make adjustments, and shift our focus and grow smartly and as needed. We can create a skills plan for you; skills are learned. Find the good instructors who can communicate and transfer knowledge. **It's not about screaming instructors within REAL; it's about providing you the best possible environment and the best instructors to help you achieve your optimal self, to enhance your practical knowledge base. It's about building, not breaking down.**

REAL Relationships - Relationships are critical and at the core of resilience. We all need support. As important as your relationship is with yourself, no one can be a lone operator for long. We need spirituality because it gives us hope, a structure within which to share and be supported. We need family, for better or worse, as we develop as individuals. *Sometimes family is the greatest challenge – so we rely on the family we choose instead of the family we are given. That's ok.* And as our relationships mature, we find spouses or partners and rely heavily on them. **You have the responsibility to nurture and protect the relationships. They are your support. They are your future. Relationships. Gotta love them. Gotta hate them. But we all need them.**

Family Readiness
Within the Family and Business Units – the one critical common thread is communication. Within each of those units there are numerous individuals who need to be included, talked to, elicited from, shared with . . . their data needs to be your data and vice versa. **COMMUNICATION.** It is key to any tactical unit, any strategic unit. It is critical to resilience of the family and business units. As mentioned before, practicing the right communication skills within the right channel, at the right time, for the right audience, is key.

REAL Awareness – In addition to the personal aspects of resilience and awareness, this extends to your children, your spouse, and your parents or whoever is in your "family" unit. Perhaps you now need to be aware of what's going on around your children's school(s). What's happening at your spouse's place of work? How are things at the nursing home with your elderly parents? Life is a balancing act, and sometimes tough, but we cannot stick our heads in the ground and hope it goes away. We are not cowards – it's adversity, we face it and stay vigilant. We deal with it. **Awareness gets complicated for the head of household – regardless of gender and situation, but if each of the individuals in the family is aware, then sharing and communicating that information becomes the most important piece.**

REAL Mindset – As your family unit talks about resilience, as you begin to broach the topics, communication is key. But you really need to dive into the concept of mindset. Do you want your children to be winners or participants in society? Everyone gets a trophy was a thing for a while. Gen Z appears to be changing that, and they are developing as a hard-charging generation. Millennials grew up differently, in a different world, and are highly developed, highly technical, highly social. And BOTH generations are getting a full dose of what it means to be resilient in 2020 with the COVID-19 global pandemic, economic distress, race riots, and unrest leading up to the election. As we get older our mindsets can become less flexible. **Make the changes with your family. What is the mindset? Make it an adventure. Make it fun. Make it purposeful. Survive and thrive as a family unit.**

REAL Fitness –Seeking emotional and physical fitness objectives as a family can be fun and wildly varied. Let's go – get outside. Be active. Keep moving as you get older. As we move out of our highly active teens, twenties, thirties, and into our forties – our bodies change; we need to focus on wellness, sustainment, maintenance (emotional and mental). **Nutrition and health become the focus as we enter parenthood and then middle age, and just staying mobile becomes more and more** critical as we age. Include the family in your movement, your mindfulness. Be well, make it a daily thing.

♻ *REAL* Skills – Within a family skills can be addressed at the individual level. But the skill set of the family as a whole will benefit as family members mature and begin to show interests in specific things. As if we were building a special forces team, we can also nurture different skill sets within a family. Someone may be very good with technology, another great with medicine. Perhaps cooking is left to the father, while home defense is a better fit with the mother who was in the armed forces. Perhaps firearms are not in your interest, perhaps living off the grid isn't either – community and gardening may be a role that makes more sense for you within your family unit. Roles may come naturally. Some may feel like a square peg in a round hole. **Go with what works for you and your family. Less rigid – more fluid . . . but seek competency and breadth on a variety of practical, survival, purposeful skills.**

👥 *REAL* Relationships – Family relationships are tough. Start by doing things as a unit. Support each other. Expand your children's experiences in the neighborhood. Volunteering, religious groups, boys/girls clubs, and youth groups offer valuable opportunities to foster an early understanding of others in the community. It is important to open the aperture enough to engage groups that are outside of your generation, or demographic – helping out at nursing homes, Special Olympics, and urban areas/homeless shelters, etc. These can be extremely enlightening. **We must nurture the relationships that are positive, constructive and purposeful. We must try to fix those that are broken, and jettison those that negatively influence our lives and are contradictory to the ultimate goal.**

Business Preparedness

As in the family unit we also must focus on communications in the business unit. Whether you are a sole proprietor or entrepreneur, a CEO of a corporation with hundreds or thousands of employees, or run the neighborhood grocery store – communication is critical.

Another core concept within this unit is a basic understanding of **business principles, profit and loss, sales, delivery, and supply and demand.** If you don't get these concepts – you will struggle with this unit. If you have not mastered these concepts – or don't have this skill set within your immediate advisors – that might be the first skill you have to acquire. Perhaps you are the visionary for your startup. It's critical you understand these fundamentals so that you CAN communicate with your team

👁 *REAL* Awareness – As we get into the business unit, awareness takes on a slightly different form in that you need to understand factors that would influence your business (much like they would at the personal or family level). Awareness of your strengths (people and skills), weaknesses (resources or talent), opportunities (for growth, capacity building, reputation building, marketing, sales), as well as threats (competition, economic downturn, change in tastes or client needs/desires) . . . **yes, it looks a lot like a SWOT chart, the typical business quad-chart that addresses Strengths, Weaknesses, Opportunities, and Threats. Also include cash position, monthly burn, business processes, and tripwires.**

🧠 *REAL* Mindset – Are you a business that's poised for growth? Have you been doing this for a while? Are you a hunter? Are you a gatherer? Are you a cost center or a profit center? What is your mindset in your job? Much may depend on your personal makeup, how you were raised, what specific skills you possess and the function you play in the business. We are not all CEOs, some are accountants in a support role, HR in a talent sustainment role, or perhaps sales and client persuasion. Know your mindset – are you heavily invested in supporting your peers and C-suite? That's great! It's needed. **Go around the room and have each key leader write down where the company is going – what's the strategy for 2021 for the company? Are they all on the same sheet?**

🏃 *REAL* Fitness – Is your business fit? What does the **morale** look like among your employees? **Is your C-suite aligned** with your strategic goals or are they unknowingly (or willfully) paddling in the wrong direction from the CEO? What does **your culture** look like? Have you taken some time to think about culture? **WHY are you all here doing what you do?** What does your company do? WHO do you and your employees want to be known as . . . WHAT do you believe in? **Are you profitable?** Is this a lifestyle company or are you driven to build and sell? **What's the pipeline look like?** Do you have **good talent**? Is your **team excited** about coming to work each day? **Are you leading a socially responsible group** of people? Have you paid attention to who you hired and what they want? **Let's take the PT test for the business.**

⚙️ *REAL* Skills – You need a visionary. Who is the dreamer driving the big picture and new ideas? You need an integrator, someone who can put the pieces together – sales, management, delivery. Business skills in the business come down to those three core areas. The more complex and depending on the type of business the more roles you will be able to describe and add to the mix. But – at the core you need to have a vision, you need someone to make it, sell it, and deliver it. Whatever IT is. Let's look at the core needs in your business. Is someone minding each one as a singular or at least major focus? If so, are they the right ones for the job? Are some people wearing multiple hats? Does that dilute the effort that is going into that key element? Sure, it does. **Let's get a skill check on the business, what seats are around the table, and who is wearing what hats.**

👥 *REAL* Relationships – Business relationships are varied and incredibly important. They range from salesperson to client; from CEO to employee; from board member to CEO; from CEO to CEO in peer groups; CEO to other C-suite in strategic leadership; from peer to peer at the line; from manager to subordinate; and from corporation to employees; and from company to community. We must ensure each are nurtured;

that they are supported with clear, quality communication. Bad relationships at any of those levels can be cancerous and destructive. Having the wrong person on board can scuttle the ship. **What's your relationship quotient? Are yours healthy? You undoubtedly know the bad ones – they are almost always in your face. They keep you up at night. They hurt the business – either directly or indirectly.**

What unit faces which Jackals? As an individual you will face certain Jackals, and some of those may translate to concerns for the family as well. Certainly, economic challenges, home defense, medical issues, and security while traveling all can affect both units.

How do those Jackals compare with those of the business? Cash flow, staffing levels, sources of capital, demand for services, raw materials and supply chain – how will you handle those?

The 3 Units represent the different ways in which our lives are lived – as individuals, within our families, and as executives, or leaders of our livelihood.

There is overlap among the pillars and units, but that's a good thing. Don't fight it.

You must apply the 5 Pillars to each of the Units. Aspire to make all 3 Units fully supported with the pillars.

7

HOW TO FOSTER RESILIENCY

People can develop resilience. It is a known fact and has been studied by scientists, and universities. Our REAL concepts are aligned with studies and reputable groups – and are supported by studies conducted by reputable groups, social scientists, psychologists, psychiatrists, and the U.S. Government and military. When we began studying resilience, talking about it, reading about it, we found that many had addressed this in studies and papers, as well as wellness groups and psychologists and psychiatrists.

For example, the American Psychological Association (APA) has identified 10 ways to develop individual resilience, and we have taken their concepts and put them in the context of our REAL system.

❶ Make connections

Human beings need to be around other human beings and animals. Communications, shared experiences (good and bad), and the ability to relate to others is critical in filling the data set. This is the data set from which we draw the ability to establish plans; understand the environment in which people find themselves; and make critical decisions about what actions to take next. **We must build relationships that matter and REAL relationships come out of these connections.**

❷ Avoid seeing crises as insurmountable problems

The world is a dangerous place, but it's important not to jump to catastrophic thinking and doomsday attitudes, but to think more positively about the opportunity that may be created by the crisis. It may be an opportunity to demonstrate skills, to progress one's career, to help another human being, to save another person's life.

Crises are inherently difficult, and usually consist of new conditions that are brought on by undesired events. But although they may be undesired, they may also create opportunities to manage oneself or those around them into a new reality.

Use the **REAL Mindset to see the world positively, as achievable, and – as recoverable when things go wrong – as a playground with unlimited possibilities.** Yes, it can be daunting – but in the end, YOU can make your path – and YOU will survive and thrive.

❸ Accept that change is a part of living

If an individual is not addressing the changes going on around them, then they are not progressing, living, and evolving. Other than the speed of light in a vacuum, change is the only constant in the world. It's critical to the person seeking more resilience to accept that many things will change in the course of a day – your schedule, the weather, relationships, and thousands of other variables over which we wield no control. Embrace the change – be ready for it, adapt. **REAL awareness REQUIRES you to understand reality. And the reality is that things must change.** Nothing in our physical world stays the same in the long run. Be adaptable – and this dovetails into REAL Mindset.

❹ Move toward your goals

While it's important to move toward your goals – be sure you have set them in the first place. Your goals need to be set with the SMART concept – they should be Specific, they should be Measurable and Attainable, Relevant, and Time-bound. Once you have set them – either in written form, or with a friend, spouse or business associate – then be sure you move towards those goals every day. Make progress.

Put your goals into context, apply your **REAL Mindset**, and get on with your life – achieving what you, your family, and your business need to be resilient.

❺ Take decisive action

It's easy to get bogged down in the thinking traps that were mentioned before. Yes, it's important to analyze the information available to you. It is important to seek information to fill the gaps that you have in your reality. However, at some point a decision must be made – with the information you have. Waiting and further deliberating, at some point no longer is beneficial – and knowing when you have enough information is sometimes a critical skill in the world that we live in. Get enough information, analyze it – and if further information is not expected soon – make the decision and drive on. **Back to REAL Mindset and Awareness – both play into taking decisive action.**

❻ Look for opportunities for self-discovery

Getting outdoors and into new environments allows us to experience completely different activities that inform what we like and don't like. When discussing career options for new employees it's often telling that very few of them know what options are available, much less what they want to aspire to achieve in their professional lives. It's critical to find opportunities to learn more about yourself, what you enjoy and what experiences and goals you want to work towards. **Adding REAL Skills to your toolkit of life.** Get outside and learn, be curious, and fit.

❼ Nurture a positive view of yourself

Social media tends to create environments and feelings of self-doubt. Individuals are constantly bombarded by digital stimuli that create an artificially high standard of what a child or human being should be, relative to their peers.

❝

"It's important to accept yourself for who you are, and to work to better yourself with reasonable and achievable goals. It's great to have lofty targets, one should shoot for the stars."

— Kris Coleman

❞

However, when social media communicates that achieving super model status is the norm – it's critical that today's developing adults know and accept this simply isn't realistic. REAL Awareness and REAL Fitness play directly into this idea. **Being aware of yourself is key. Apply techniques to improve your self-confidence and understanding of how you are viewed among your REAL Relationships.**

❽ Keep things in perspective

Is this a crisis or a minor setback? Is this a long-term problem or a short-term issue? How bad is it? How good is it? Perspective is key – it's key to reality, and reality allows you to move towards greater resilience because your expectations are managed, and you are dealing with realistic phenomena – not altered realities, unrealistic hopes, and pipe dreams. Ask someone to confirm what you are thinking and be your sounding board. See if what you think is happening is in agreement with their perspective. As life gets more complicated, as we age, as we change jobs, and start long-term relationships it's critical that we maintain perspective. **Back to REAL Awareness and REAL Relationships . . . where are you in life, what is your reality, what information is coming in that you can trust that isn't biased or misleading.**

❾ Maintain a hopeful outlook

Understanding what reality is, has proved to be a critical area where today's young people struggle to keep things in perspective. And when things are no longer in perspective it's easy to become disheartened and lose hope in attaining your goals. **Having a REAL Mindset is key here. One cannot be a hopeless optimist, but viewing life in a positive light is hugely helpful.**

⑩ Take care of yourself

Eating right, getting enough quality sleep, and exercising are all important aspects of wellness. If you want to grow, progress, evolve into a more resilient person – you cannot at the same time ignore these key areas. Wellness is critical to your development as a resilient person. **REAL Fitness – emotional and physical – is key to building an elastic self that can bounce back from stress and setbacks.**

Being flexible

Resilience involves maintaining flexibility and balance in your life as you deal with stressful circumstances and traumatic events. This happens in several ways, including:

- Letting yourself experience strong emotions, and also realizing when you may need to avoid experiencing them at times in order to continue functioning.

- You cannot expect things to remain constant – change is normal, and therefore your flexibility is essential.

- Stepping forward and taking action to deal with your problems and meet the demands of daily living, and also stepping back to rest and reenergize yourself.

- Spending time with loved ones to gain support and encouragement, and also nurturing yourself.

- Relying on others, and also relying on yourself.

Growth and learning are key to developing a resilient lifestyle. We need a grasp on reality and when we stop learning, our version of reality begins to stagnate. Children require learning, humans must keep learning.

> "Gritty people have a growth mindset; when bad things happen, they don't give up"
> — Angela Duckworth, author of *Grit: The Power of Passion and Perseverance.*

Not only do they need an interest, a goal, a passion – but they must continue to grow to keep that passion firmly rooted in the reality around them. Grit and resilience are learnable and consist of constructive behaviors and skills.

Duckworth and Michael Matthews conducted a study in 2019 that analyzed 11,258 West Point cadets over 10 years. While they looked at a mix of traits – GPA, physical fitness, IQ, training, graduation rates – grit was the highlight. Grit in the study clarified that it is about having a "fire in your belly" to persevere over time and with a deep interest in achieving the goal. Cadets worked hard to get into West Point for years prior, and then once in had to continue achieving in order to successfully graduate.

Cadets in most cases got into a "flow" – peak enjoyment, focus, and performance combined to create an optimal experience. Being totally absorbed by the process or task at hand, or flow, is also described by professional athletes, super marathoners, and special forces operators. When you get into the flow of using tactics to rescue a hostage, working with a team, under pressure, using your surprise, speed, and violence of action to win the day – you get into a very focused flow. It's short-term, but very intense and rewarding.

It's not always a short-term thing as Matthews and Duckworth found, but realistically for many people it might be months or years' worth of grit and flow.

Part of the challenge is that we are ignoring the real world around us – walking and falling into fountains as we stare at our phones, or driving off the road because we just received a new social media endorsement or a funny photo from a friend. Staring at our screens tells others we are not in the moment,

we are not worthy of their attention, and we are sitting ducks for predators. Being preyed upon doesn't help our resiliency. It helps the Jackals.

Pay attention to your surroundings, get back into reality.

Apply the 5 pillars. Foster your resilience.

Get outside. Experience life. Grow. Learn.

WHO NEEDS RESILIENCY?

Organizations are typically resilient because the leader has determined that the organization needs to be resilient. He or she sets the tone, and the way forward. If the leader, however, doesn't see the value, the need to invest in resiliency, continuity planning, contingency thinking, etc., then the organization will struggle to survive and thrive. The organizational body will likely take the path of least resistance, and happily just "be" instead of being resilient.

Who needs to be resilient? All business owners. All mayors, governors, presidents. All parents. Those are the leaders of our communities. And when one of those isn't, the rest of that community pays the price. And when the community responds to a failed leader who has proven their lack of resilience, that leadership vacuum will be filled with someone with resilient qualities. If you want to be ready for the call to help your organization, your family, your business, your community, your country – become resilient. Everyone can benefit from resilience – but again, it starts with the individual – with personal resilience.

Although it's personal, I would argue that resilience is a national security matter, that all individuals in the U.S. should strive to be resilient. Be a good citizen, make our country stronger, be more resilient – for you, for your family, for your country.

If we apply the REAL system to the construct of national security, we find it fits nicely – like a bespoke outfit. But it hasn't been an outfit that politicians and pundits like to push and endorse. Resilient people are not easy to manipulate. Resilient people are based in reality, taking in multiple streams of information, analyzing it all for their consumption to make informed decisions. The informed citizen is a resilient person.

As a nation, our country is facing Jackals on many fronts – both foreign and domestic. On a daily basis the country's infrastructure, economy, military, and national security agencies are being attacked on the cyber front. We are facing enemies in the proliferation of weapons of mass destruction, upheaval in the Middle East, as well as threats from the Far East, and against our allies in Europe and around the world.

Domestically, we are facing the aforementioned challenges of civil unrest, equality, and injustice – all while battling a global pandemic and massive unemployment. It will take us years to recover from these Jackals, but we cannot let our guard down as we confront these domestic issues . . . or the international Jackals will take advantage.

Our military, our navy, our astronauts – our protectors – remain some of the more resilient people today because they must expect change. Their conditions are harsher; and their conditions could kill them during a normal day. They are trained to be more resilient – to think on their feet, to expect the unexpected. Weather, air quality, and unexpected threats to their lives can manifest instantly. Their ability to think on their feet helps the crew of the International Space Station. A shipmate's skills provide resilience value to their captain and their crewmates.

Resilience in individuals made the U.S. what it is today. Resilience in our citizens and communities will be what helps the U.S. get through the next great challenge – whatever that may be. Regardless of your race, your geography, or origin, resilience will be what carries our species back to the moon, to Mars, into the stars and beyond.

Great companies are full of resilient, adaptable people who can adjust for changing conditions. These organizations understand the need for:

- ➤ Preparedness
- ➤ Urgent decision making
- ➤ Realistic perspectives
- ➤ Flexibility
- ➤ Fitness and grit

The pandemic of 2020 began to sort out the wheat from the chaff in the business community. Those who were prepared, survived and thrived. Those who were less prepared may have survived but did not flourish, and it remains to be seen if they will catapult out of the recovery and into prosperity.

Organizations must also embrace the 5-3-1 System to become resilient and apply the pillars to each individual division with the business. One must ask the Sales Division to have redundancies in their relationships so that sales opportunities aren't missed. The CEO must ensure that those in the C-suite back each other up, that their approaches to their areas of responsibility are aligned to the one strategic goal. This takes communication and REAL Relationship management. Having a management dashboard with measurable and pertinent data supports REAL Awareness.

The CFO must pay dogged attention to the resources and ensure that the company is following a REAL Fitness regimen from a fiscal perspective. Is the pipeline based in reality? Are the fiscal decisions being made in a conservative fashion that promotes a healthy bottom line? Costs have to be managed.

Organizations need to live and breathe resilience. And organizations are not just simple organisms, they can be made up of multiple and varied modules. Companies have divisions. Private families have Family Offices, or charitable family foundations. Each of these is to be considered its own organization, needing its own flavor and intensity of resilience that is tailored to its needs, its scale, its necessity to the rest of the organization.

Ideally, resilience becomes an unconscious competency, where you only really think about it when it hits the fan and the Continuity of Operations Plan must be enacted. If an organization brings the 5-3-1 System into its DNA, only then does it become part of the organization and the benefits can be fully realized.

Individuals, families and businesses ALL require resilience in today's hyperconnected and dynamic world.

Some have it and most will achieve it if they pursue the 5 Pillars.

9

LEADERSHIP VS. RESILIENCY

Personal resiliency is the cornerstone of this effort. Individuals make up families and businesses. Families and businesses need leaders, as does any group trying to achieve specific goals.

Some think that leaders are naturally resilient. There are many examples of people who were leaders until the adversity hit. Many movies have been produced that show a leader failing at the task, only for their shoes to be filled by the underdog – the unexpected leader, the hero to rise from the ashes.

Leaders need resilience. Leadership, like resilience can also be taught. Good leadership schools discuss, practice, and even drill scenarios that require the developing leaders to demonstrate their resilience skills. Scouts, first responders, law enforcement, firefighters all must understand that concept of resilience – but that's not usually how it's taught. Officer Safety and Survival, Incident Command, wilderness medicine, survival skills are all taught – and correctly so. But, in the end it's rare that we talk about resilience. It's rare that we understand how the concept applies to people.

> **Great Leaders Know Resiliency**
>
> This statement is validated by the life of our 26th President, Theodore Roosevelt. His early childhood was plagued with severe asthma, poor eyesight and was often referred to as a "weak child," until his father took the extraordinary steps to place him and other children on an exercise regime. This action along with on-going encouragement provided Roosevelt the necessary attributes of resiliency which he later termed, "The Strenuous Life." In a 1899 speech he delivered to an audience in Chicago, he described the Strenuous Life (Resiliency), *".....I wish to preach, not the doctrine of ignoble ease, but the doctrine of the strenuous life, the life of toil and effort, of labor and strife; to preach that highest form of success which comes, not to the man who desires mere easy peace, but to the man who does not shrink from danger, from hardship, or from bitter toil, and who out of these wins the splendid ultimate triumph."* The transformation from a fragile childhood to a leader as a soldier, conservationist, statesman and President was achieved through ability to overcome challenges and dedicate himself to a life built on resiliency.
>
> —Nick Nicholson, PhD, FBI Academy Leadership Instructor (retired), Adjunct Professor, University of Virginia

Our military academies —West Point, The Naval Academy, The Air Force Academy, The Coast Guard Academy, The Merchant Marine Academy, and similar U.S. military training institutions drill our military minds in resilience. They are required day in and day out to think about the challenges ahead, to assess the possibilities, to understand the risks, think clearly and critically about the realities they are facing, and then to take decisive action.

The Star Trek movie series even has a classic scene where Captain Kirk faces "death" in a Starfleet Academy training scenario. It was important for Starfleet cadets to experience the Kobayashi Maru . . . the "no-win" scenario. However, Captain Kirk found the scenario wanting. He doesn't like to lose. Therefore, he changed the conditions of the test to find a way around the "no-win" scenario. Whether you are a Picard fan or a Kirk fan – you can see and appreciate the path to resilience in that movie scene.

Resiliency Can Be Taught

It's true that some people are born leaders. It's also true that some are born resilient. But it's rare that people become specialists in leadership. They have it, they demonstrate it, but it's rare that it is characterized as a profession.

The same goes for resilience. People have it. Some are born with it. Many learn it. But it's rare that people turn to each other and say – "man, you really are a resilient person." Or "You have quite the resilience quotient." You don't have to be resilient to get through this world. And you don't have to be resilient to be put into a leadership role – but it sure helps. And as a leader, you don't have to be resilient – but as a leader without it, do not expect to stay in the position of leadership after your first crisis.

Who's more resilient? Picard or Kirk?

Sources: https://www.digitalspy.com/movies/a470566/star-trek-5-of-captain-kirks-most-memorable-alien-loves/

https://memory-alpha.fandom.com/wiki/Jean-Luc_Picard

Good characteristics of leaders include inspiration, motivation, anticipation, emotional intelligence, and realism. There are others – empathy, intelligence, vision, decision making. But for the resilience discussion – anticipation, emotional intelligence, and realism are keystones for good leaders that also demonstrate resilient qualities. **Many of these can be found in our 5 pillars of resilience – REAL Awareness, REAL Mindset, REAL Fitness, REAL Skills and REAL Relationships. All have overlapping elements of these key characteristics of leaders.**

The Art of Anticipation

Anticipation means that you have enough data to make an informed forecast. A good executive administrator can anticipate what the CEO needs the next day, perhaps even before the CEO herself understands the conditions under which they will need to operate. Knowing what meetings have been confirmed, and which ones have slipped to the right on the calendar is critical to understanding how the CEO will get to eat lunch; what personal errands might be accomplished if work ends early; or if that Vice President can squeeze in that five minute chat with the CEO between calls.

In sport, anticipation becomes crucial to achieving short term goals, like scoring points, passing another race car driver, getting that first down, or ensuring your team is ready to defend against the next offensive move. In baseball, players in the field are coached to anticipate what they will need to do with the ball if it were hit to them. If there is a runner on first and third for instance, and the ball is hit to the second baseman – what should the second baseman anticipate doing with the ball? The same can apply to basketball and soccer. What opportunities exist by taking a specific action as the team breaks towards the goal in an attempt to score? Could the ball be passed to you for a scoring attempt? You should be positioning yourself for a rebound, or where you think the ball will be next.

Resilient people must apply their realistic view of the world to the opportunities that present themselves in anticipation of other events.

As a virus begins to cross borders and additional breakouts occur, should a CEO and his team be anticipating limiting business travel? Should the CEO be paying attention to the health situation for his family? What preparations are in place?

If the CEO is a naturally resilient person, these kinds of ideas come naturally to her as conditions change. If the CEO is not resilient as an individual, or thinks they are but does not have a realistic view (e.g., the pandemic will never reach our area), will the company be as prepared as it needs to be? Will his/her family be prepared? Perhaps another person will fill the lane, anticipate the need, and position themselves with helpful information and experience – based on their realistic view of the world. REAL Awareness fosters anticipation.

Harnessing Emotional Intelligence

Emotional intelligence and awareness can play a large role in an individual's resilience. It is imperative that the resilient person has the capacity to adjust their emotions, keep them in check as needed, when conditions change dramatically. It is thought that senior leadership will be emotionally compromised when family crises manifest. Whether it's a distraction due to a family illness, or perhaps the kidnapping of a key employee, or perhaps an emotional conflict of interest as business needs begin to supersede those of the family.

Resilient persons have the capacity to realistically adjust their responses, or hand those responsibilities off to others when they become emotionally compromised. An individual's emotional intelligence quotient has an impact on their perspective of their reality. If they are making decisions based on emotions, instead of a clinical, real view of the world, it can result in poor judgment. A high level of emotional intelligence means a person can put their emotions in check during certain situations, and reduce the possibility of a rash decision that may not be based on precise conditions. The situation may look very different to someone who is not emotionally connected to the situation. Having a higher level of emotional intelligence enhances their view of reality – the next important factor of a leader.

Stay Rooted in Reality

Reality, as you now know from reading, plays a key role in resilience. If an individual is operating on information that is tainted by emotion or skewed by a false sense of the current state of affairs, or is otherwise untrue, it will be difficult for that person to understand the boundaries for responses to crises. It will be difficult for that person to make appropriate contingency plans, and challenging for them to accept the difficulty that may lie ahead for him/her and their loved ones.

The resilient person has a clinical view of the situation and is able to make unemotional decisions about what needs to be done to bounce back from adversity. They are able to judge accurately the possibilities for action that lie ahead. They are less likely to forego decisions that could help them due to their misunderstanding of the current state of affairs. Are you aware of your reality?

Our Past is Always Present

Different people have had different experiences as they grow up. Those experiences are REAL and will form their emotional intelligence, help them understand and perhaps develop an ability to anticipate, and immerse them in different levels of reality. We all know people who have grown up in sheltered environments. These individuals have not had to face adversity, not had to make decisions that impact their family or future – and, we know this to be true because of what they say, and how they declare their environments to be.

As individuals, executives, and leaders reflect on their resiliency, they should take into account previous experiences – their upbringing, challenges they have faced, and how they handled them. This informs their REAL Awareness, bases them in reality.

- [ ] Have you worked hard and overcome challenges to get where you are?
- [ ] Have your decisions in the past been based in reality?
- [ ] How did those decisions work out?
- [ ] Were you surprised by certain developments at work or among close friends?

54

- [ ] Could you have anticipated those events?
- [ ] Why didn't you see some things coming? A relationship breakup? A termination of employment?
- [ ] Would others consider you "clueless" about your situation? Blinded by love?
- [ ] Were you clinical about those decisions or were they jaded by personal biases or feelings about others that were involved?
- [ ] What would you have done differently?

Today's leaders should take personal stock of their resiliency...

- [ ] Did you get where you are because of a family legacy?
- [ ] Did your family's affluence play a part in your achieving a certain level of status?
- [ ] Have you traveled the world?
- [ ] Have you worked among other cultures?
- [ ] Can you speak another language?
- [ ] Do you pay attention to current events?
- [ ] What other aspects can help you solidify your reality?
- [ ] If so, what can you do to increase your resiliency?

The Jackals we have seen in the past are real, and could return. It is a choice if we decide to submit. **It is imperative that we learn from those Jackals, but not empower them or give them power over us psychologically or emotionally.**

There are lessons in our past. We should explore them but NOT relive them or wallow in that historical morass of things gone by. But if you have not explored the lessons that are to be learned from past adversity, past challenges, employments and relationships gone bad – individuals are missing out on good opportunities to learn emotionally, adjust the standard for reality, and be really ready for the next time the ball is hit to you.

This is a Resiliency Audit . . .

. . . and it can be applied to all of the units. It starts, as we have said from the beginning, with the individual – whether a business leader, religious leader, political leader, family leader, or head of household. It's good to take stock of your resiliency.

REAL Awareness, REAL Mindset, REAL Fitness, REAL Skills and REAL Relationships all have measurable facets and quantities that should be audited from time to time, whether formally or informally. We can look back after a traumatic event, a family illness, death of a friend, or bankruptcy. Any major life event can inform our future – make us stronger, present another opportunity to LEARN and inform our reality.

Resiliency is key to good leader's success. It can be learned.

Actively practice anticipation of threats and risks. It's not paranoia, it's practical application of risk anticipation.

Emotional intelligence helps keep leaders grounded.

Learn from past mistakes but don't dwell in their negativity. Look at them clinically.

Do a Resiliency Audit for your family or business today. Get ahead of the Jackals.

PERSONAL RESILIENCY

Why are you reading this book? Why take the time? Why, indeed.

You are reading this because you have doubt and you want to improve. **You are being proactive.** And, you want to clear that doubt and fill the knowledge gap with REAL skills that will help you. **You have a desire to improve your three units – yourself, your family, and your business. That is the WHY.** You have been working your way through a tough year, personally, financially, emotionally, for you and your family, and your business. The WHY is self-evident. You CAN deal with adversity – you can face it. You can be better.

And now that we are clear on the WHY – let's talk about WHAT we will do and HOW we will get there, for you and your family, and your livelihood.

Resilience Tools

There are tools available to us to help us proactively prepare for adversity. This is not unlike what law enforcement, the military, first responders go through in their training. The training has been developed over decades to ensure an officer's safety, a paramedic's effectiveness, and a soldier's discipline and resilience.

We touched on a resiliency audit in the last chapter and this takes us squarely into the proactive tool for self-awareness, and a battery of questions to better understand where we stand, in reality, vis-à-vis our situation.

Our tool for REAL Awareness lies in our ability to reflect on past experiences and what personal challenges can help you learn about what you need to do to build resilience.

By exploring answers to the following questions about yourself and your reactions to challenging life events, you may discover how you can better respond to difficult situations in your life. Consider the following:

- What kinds of events have been most difficult for me?
- How have those events typically affected me, my family, and my business?
- Who do I turn to as important people in my life when I am faced with a challenge?
- To whom have I reached out for support when faced with a traumatic or stressful experience?
- Over the years what have I learned about myself during times of adversity?
- Have I been able to help others in a similar experience?
- How has that interaction with others helped me grow?
- Have I been able to overcome obstacles, and if so, how?
- What actions make me more optimistic about the future?

Self-awareness is key, but knowing what and who is around you – the status of your situation and "seeing" what is about to unfold before it happens to you is critical. Observation skills, situational awareness, attack recognition, and personal security are fundamental skills for resilient people in today's world.

If you are not aware of the Jackals at your doorstep, down the street at the next intersection, or lurking around your weak bank account, you will be surprised when they attack. And with a 90 percent success rate with surprise on their side, the Jackals will always have the advantage. Be aware and take away the Jackals' advantage. Don't passively choose to be a victim.

Formal training is how some of the most resilient people in the world achieve their elasticity. They chose careers and vocations that put them through formalized training curriculum, and perhaps even a crucible of physical and mental challenges to catalyze their transformation.

For resilience, formal training is available across all five pillars and for all three units. REAL training makes experiential based learning available to our participants. From virtual training, while we work and live remotely, to bespoke training for private families, as well as face to face, destination training with some of the best instructors in the world. REAL training carries the themes and the system from the Personal Resiliency exercises through to the more tactical Family Readiness; and, into the most complex Business Preparedness issues.

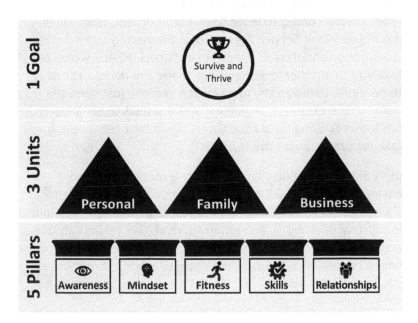

There are exercises available to enhance REAL Awareness through situational awareness and observation skills; self-awareness practices and methods; and complex scenarios for the executive or family business leader that test and validate approaches, plans, and preparations that were well-intentioned.

For REAL Mindset, those tests are a common thread throughout all the various trainings available. Each class you experience should address mindset, adjusting it – reinforcing it. Your attitude and your mental stance are critical to whatever activity you are undertaking, whether it is sports, sewing, accounting, studying, playing music, charging that hill, investigating a threat, saving a life – or most importantly the proactive and reactive skills needed for you, your family and your business to survive and thrive. It all comes back around.

For REAL Skills – this is where the rubber meets the road. Practical skills applied in your daily life plucked literally from the curriculum and principles of instruction of some of the most skilled, successful operators in the U.S. government. From Special Forces, to federal law enforcement, from military medics to Secret Service agents, from firemen to pilots, from competition shooters to intelligence officers. REAL training can take you to another level. You have made the decision already to be more, to live more, to go for it. Now you just need the training, the experiential practice and the tests to establish the fundamentals and build from there. It will take repetition; it will take experts to guide you through it.

REAL Skills include first aid, automotive mechanics, land navigation, driving, self-defense, home defense for the family, shelter construction, living in the outdoors, making a fire, finding food, rural operations, and urban survival. Our teams can take you places you could never go before, to achieve skill levels you haven't experienced – or for the more seasoned, experiences you haven't had lately.

We believe in stress inoculation, immersing our participants in artificially stressful environments that work towards adding a specific skill (or skills) so that individuals can be tested under the right conditions, with realism. These are significant stressors that impact all the senses, raise the level of fear and adrenaline, and do so in a realistic environment – sometimes with role players, and always with intensity.

Source: Angela Hays Photography

Training should be done in a constructive environment, preferably outside the classroom in a realistic environment. There's no need for screaming or yelling as instruction, perhaps for atmospherics if the scenario wants. However, once the adult has committed to adding skills, it's about learning as professional adults. Perhaps we provide the fundamental skills needed to protect your residence – but then we run participants through scenario after scenario with a real intruder, in the dark, with different layouts to present those learners real decisions to make under stress. The participants get to learn from hearing, watching, doing, and receiving constructive feedback.

When to be Reactive
Having a crisis means that there is a threat, there is an element of surprise, there is a short timeline to remedy the problem, and a possibility that there may require a change in the future to prevent this from happening again.

Key elements of crisis management include: understanding the problem, addressing immediate needs, resourcing for urgent needs, and handling the message and resolution smartly and quickly.

Ideally you have a crisis management plan, an emergency action plan, or perhaps a business continuity plan so that you know your threats, and you expect them. You should have a team ready to deal with them – one with structure, experience with the plan, and clearly defined roles. And one should know what's needed to step into the threat, manage the response, and deal effectively with the communications and after-effects.

Individuals can have their own means of dealing with crises and have "informal" crisis plans in their heads. Family planning can range from a parental approach with checklists, to familial practice of fire escapes at the home, and Go-Bag for escaping the area. Business crisis plans should include a written document that is updated regularly, addresses a myriad of threats and hazards, and ensures the brand and business processes and assets are protected.

The Cool-Hand Approach

During high school I managed to acquire the nickname of Coolhand. This wasn't based on popularity, and definitely not on good looks nor slick demeanor. It was, however, based on the way I handled things when a situation went poorly. When the cops were showing up, when friends needed assistance, when we experienced loss, frustration or a major setback, my duty, I felt, was to help in any way I could. So, when others were yelling and screaming, running away and hiding, or swallowed by despair and frozen by fear – I tried very hard to have a cool head, to approach things with a steady hand.

Approaching things clinically may be critical to handling them in a way that results in success. Emotions, anxiety, and fear can all affect the outcome of your important decisions while under stress. If you can look at the situation clinically – without bias or emotion – it can help you manage the situation.

Being decisive is important and can be the difference between life and death when things go bad quickly and violently.

> **❝**
>
> General Patton said, "A good plan violently executed right now is better than a perfect plan executed next week."
>
> Voltaire is paraphrased as having said, "don't let perfect be the enemy of the good."
>
> **❞**

What I've practiced time and time again with my government colleagues overseas in dangerous locations . . . just move. Get off the "X."

> Many of my colleagues have been through the security training, of one 3-letter agency or another (CIA, FBI, NSA, etc.) where the key to surviving a critical incident is simply "moving." If there is a fire in your home – get out (move). If there is an active shooter – run (move). If a pandemic is developing, don't let your business continue to spend unnecessary funds, expose your employees to the disease, and take your company down – cut your costs, have the employees work remotely, and save your company (move). Be decisive.

If there is some other adverse action developing, don't contemplate all the options, don't think deeply about what is happening, and whatever you do DO NOT just stay there and become a victim. If you freeze in place, you may die in place. Get off the X. Move. Be decisive.

Things to Practice

Whatever training you receive should take you from objectives, through fundamentals, to practical exercises and then onward to ways to improve your skills beyond the classroom and training environment. Whatever planning the parents or the CEO puts into place to protect the family or the organization should include exercises and drills.

There are many ways for individuals to practice resilience and security skills. During one's daily commute or errand running, defensive driving skills can be used almost daily. Considering situational awareness, paying attention to areas known to be more dangerous, and applying defensive driving techniques to avoid accidents are great ways for individuals to practice resiliency skills.

Businesses must exercise their leadership and their tactical execution of their continuity and emergency action plans. Tabletop exercises that are scenario based and time-driven, can provide a constructive and realistic environment to test leaders' knowledge of the plan, and its effectiveness, as well as practicality to emerging threats. Tactical drills to move employees away from the threat (into a hallway for a tornado or out to a parking lot for a fire drill) are also essential to highlight practical impediments to success. Are the emergency fire exit doors actually chained and locked to keep homeless people from entering from the outside? Are you ready to deal with a false bomb threat that pushes your employees outside and actually into a more vulnerable position that an active shooter can now prey upon? Practical exercises should test your technology and plans for recovery. Do you have the computers, software, data, and bandwidth needed to get your key employees back online and productive after a business disruption, hurricane, or cyber-attack?

But remember, practice alone doesn't make perfect. It's not enough to just do repetitions that aren't dialed into the proper form, function, and speed. But perfect practice can make for perfect skills. Don't do drills and exercises for the sake of doing them, checking a box, and telling the executives that you are compliant. Do them correctly, do them perfectly, do them often. Keep learning, never stop – you can always improve.

"Everyday Carry" is a term used by law enforcement, first responders, and in the military that reflects what these "ready" and resilient people carry every day, either on their person or in their backpack. Typically, these include things like – keys, wallet, knife, pens, flashlights, extra power source, etc.

Backpacks have grown to be Mini Go-Bag in that they also include nutrition bars, a tourniquet and first aid items, a multi-tool, water, and maybe a firearm. Depending on your environment, your job, your location, and the threat environment you are most likely to find yourself in everyday, you may want to consider what constitutes your "Everyday Carry" items.

Go-Bags

The important factor in figuring out what should go in your personal Go-Bag is do you NEED that item, and how much weight does it add to your pack. Is the extra weight worth how much you need that item to be on your person in an emergency?

Special thanks to Jeff Kirkham and Jason Ross for this basic Go-Bag list:

Red Five REAL Go-Bag List

Backpack	Underwear
Water	Socks
Water Bottle	Jacket
Purifier Straw	Rain Jacket
Protein/Energy Bars	Hat
MRE or Packaged Meal	Gloves
Spoon/Spork	Vest
Can Opener	Shoes/Boots
Stove	Emergency Blanket
Fuel	Tarp/Poncho
Shirt	Sleeping Bag
Pants	Ground Pad

Lighter	Flashlight
Matches	Batteries
Tinder	Multi-tool
Hand Warmer	Cord
Prescription Meds	Knife
OTC Kit	Packing Bags
First Aid Kit	Tool Bag
Trauma Kit	Waterproof Bags
Red 5 Go Bag Packing List	Tape
Hand Sanitizer	Trash Bags
Wet Wipes	Pepper Spray
Liquid Soap	Taser
Towel	Cash
Toilet Paper	Credit Card
Toothbrush/Paste	Keys
Sunscreen	ID
Insect Repellent	Glasses
Female Hygiene	Sunglasses
Chapstick	N95 facemask
Phone charger	Notebook
Portable Radio	Pencil
Headlamp	

As you strive to be REAL about your personal resilience:
- **Follow the 5 pillars.**
- **Establish your "Everyday Carry" items.**
- **Get training, and train with the gear you expect to carry and use.**
- **Build your Go-Bag.**

FAMILY ADVERSITY

Adversity and resiliency go hand in hand and everyone has had their moments – and that includes our families. We must work to support the second unit, the family unit, so that it can be ready for what lies ahead.

We are born into our families; we don't have a choice in that matter. Sometimes things work really well and families get along. Sometimes, as we all know, families are full of conflict. There is a reason portions of those relationships are referred to as sibling rivalries. Competition among siblings is very common. With competition comes a winner, and of course a loser – creating adversity. How each of us deals with losing is formed over the years. Winning is easy in most cases – dealing with the humbling loss is never fun, and not desired, of course. Everyone wants to win, to be good at something to be valued. When we aren't, we then must face those feelings of negativity. I say, rub some dirt on it, pick yourself up, and dust yourself off – it's not the end of the world.

As children grow up, passing through different stages of development, social growth, pressures and exploration, friction is expected. Friction and conflict occur between family members, between family members and new friends, and between parents and children. This is life. Life is what happens when you interact with mom and dad, brothers, sisters, and cousins. Parent/child relationships can be troubling, as a result of abuse (either emotional or physical), or challenged by marital issues, or a divorce. What individuals do with those experiences matters – what children internalize, process, and make part of their emotional intelligence matters. What is their reality as they perceive it?

Carol Dweck's Mindset Theory lends the concepts that there is a spectrum, and that you are somewhere between a fixed mindset and a growth mindset. Fixed is when people believe their basic qualities, their intelligence, their talents, etc. are just fixed fruits, and that they only have a certain amount. There is no additional potential available.

With REAL, we implore you to take Dweck's other path, that of a growth mindset. All aspects of your person, your talents, your abilities can be further developed over time. This occurs through experience, mentorship, and learning. This mindset is for people who "go for it!"

Mindset for children can be influenced by parents and teachers. Educators can encourage feelings of confidence and excitement that help children recover from failure. Teachers can help kids view hard work and effort as "normal," and that they should use it to solve problems that arise. Mindset can help them with confidence and encourage them to seek out challenges, set goals, and work through them instead of being worried and avoiding them.

Parents can help kids and their mindset by showing them that practice, and working on a weakness will result in progress. Minimizing the hard work does not help. Children need to know that there isn't always an easy answer. In a modern society it's become common to get the answer from your phone; with the tap of an app, the answer is presented. Life isn't like that.

Children need role models, and children need to conquer some Jackals by themselves. Set the model for them, and expose them to others who are facing adversity. Studies have shown that role models play a prominent role in children's lives, and parents are the primary influencer as role models. Consider if it's a good opportunity to be a role model for the kids.

Seeing a childhood friend go through cancer was a life-lived case study in reinforcement of resilient behavior. My friend's fight with cancer was an influence on my life. She fought through leukemia and made it to remission. But it was tough to see her go from a healthy remission back into the fight for her life. Her parents were role models for her, and my parents were role models for me. She was a fighter. And, in her memory now, looking back, she provided some inputs for me on how to keep things in perspective and be grateful.

If we are brought up in an environment where children do not experience these things, those experiences will, most certainly, be more difficult if experienced for the first time in adulthood. As many of us did, I lost several close friends to cancer, car accidents, or just moving away during adolescence. Some instances I understood better than others depending on my age and maturity. Some were clearly devastating, and were felt in the heart as well as the mind. Those experiences leave scar tissue – some of which we never lose, much of which makes us stronger.

A couple looks over the ruins of their home after a wildfire.
Source: Getty images

Maturity comes with time and experience. Maturity allows for a more experienced view of the world and reality. Life provides us with experiences that make for scar tissue, both emotional and physical and those are the result of challenges, misfortunes, misadventures, and sometimes violence. Some of those experiences are unique and leave their particular scars behind – many share traits of feelings of loss, betrayal, anger, fear, and embarrassment. Being fired leaves you embarrassed, anxious and angry. Divorces are said to be similar, along with feelings of resentment and rejection. Bankruptcies – not terribly different. And as we face the painful losses of family members through sudden, or prolonged illness – we can feel abandoned, guilty for surviving, and perhaps desperate.

Faith can play a strong part in one's resiliency around family adversity. Has the family a strong base in spirituality? Perhaps there is a religious contingent or supporters from the local church group to help the parents and kids get through the challenges they face. This is core to the REAL Relationships. Those values will inform the strength of their character, their ability to survive and thrive in the face of adversity. Are they spiritually strong? This element frequently runs as a common thread throughout a family. It is a bonding element between individuals, a common experience during childhood and into adulthood.

That said – we must endeavor to persevere as a family. Things happen in life – such as losing your job, getting a divorce, filing for bankruptcy, losing a family member, or a sudden or catastrophic illness.

Each of these scenarios bring its own disappointment, emotions, economic impact, stress, and perhaps the worst of outcomes – financial destitution, or loss of life. One can proactively prepare for some of these, but for most of the learning it comes from experience. From childhood on, we know that life can include disappointment, it can include loss, and it can include pain and suffering.

All of these aspects of family readiness apply to a family of any size, affluence, culture, or geography. For some larger families that have evolved into corporate entities, some other aspects might need additional consideration.

The 5 Pillars for a Private Family Office

As part of our REAL Awareness, REAL Mindset, REAL Fitness, REAL Skills and REAL Relationships – something particularly interesting comes to mind. It goes back to core values, and while they may be based in one's upbringing, things are different if the family is perhaps larger, extended, or perhaps formally incorporated into a Family Office for investment and support. As the family legacy, business, and affluence is taken into account there are other ways to instill values, a sense of reality, community, honor, and grit.

Grit is highlighted in the Code of the West, a topic eloquently discussed and explained to all in a book entitled, *Cowboy Ethics*, by James P. Owen, where he outlines 10 components to the Code:

1. Live Each Day with Courage
2. Take Pride in Your Work
3. Always Finish What You Start
4. Do What Has to Be Done
5. Be Tough, But Fair
6. When You Make a Promise, Keep It
7. Ride for the Brand
8. Talk Less and Say More
9. Remember That Some Things Aren't for Sale
10. Know Where to Draw the Line

While we won't get into all ten, several items highlight the resilience and the grit that the cowboys of the world possess, and have demonstrated over the centuries of their history. In the U.S., cowboys and cowboy culture evolved out of the settling of the Great and Western Plains in our early history. There was little law enforcement, wide open spaces, few support groups, bitterly challenging environments, and lots of threats and hazards to life on the open range. Cowboys had to find ways to tackle issues, eat, not die, and in the end – find a way to make an honest living. They wanted to survive and thrive, the 1 Goal. Two of the items in the Code of the West speak specifically to resilience - *Always Finish What You Start* and *Do What Has to Be Done*.

Don't quit. Even though you experience a setback – a thunderstorm scatters your herd, or a bear steals your supper – don't quit. Don't let failures or misfortune stop you from finishing what you started. If the cattle must be in Montana before August, you better not stop for long anywhere after you leave Texas. It's a long drive, fraught with danger. Don't quit. When you are riding through hell, keep riding. *Always Finish What You Start.*

❝

"To the cowboy, it was a matter of honor to do the right thing even – and especially – when the odds were fearsomely stacked against him," Owen.

❞

To the modern human being, this still holds true. While we don't ride horses in our streets anymore, and frontier justice is frowned upon, just make the right call. When the odds are stacked against you – when people are wronging you – you can fall back on doing the right thing. You won't regret it. Apply the REAL Mindset, REAL Fitness, and REAL Skills. Sticking your head in the sand, avoiding reality, skewing your reality will not serve you well in the long run. *Do What Has to Be Done.*

Much like the wild west, today's private family offices, our neighbors, and our communities can help other families with economic hardship, weather emergencies, challenging issues at school, with crime and gangs, or while addressing a pandemic. Many of the private family offices have philanthropic divisions or foundations that focus on this aspect of their culture. Neighborhoods develop a sense of community when there is quality communication, a common sense of values and perhaps even informal goals for families that live nearby. If like-minded families come together in cooperation to overcome a challenge, the bond is secured and their readiness enhanced.

Individuals make up a family, and as we have stated earlier in this book, the individual is key. The individuals' REAL Awareness and observation skills will inform the a rain, flash flooding, lightening, high winds, hail, and of course-tornadoes. wareness of the family. The individuals in the family should share a survival mentality, a REAL Mindset. The REAL Fitness of the individuals will benefit the overall well-being of the family unit. Are the individuals in the family emotionally stable, with their perspectives based in reality? The REAL Skills, aggregated among the individuals constitute the broader skill set that benefits the family readiness level. And lastly, and likely the most important in the end – the REAL Relationships that make up the interactions, the love, the respect, the cooperation and sacrifice among the family members will carry the day.

Each individual's personal resilience, their REAL 5 pillars of resilience, will create a Family Readiness *greater than its individual parts*.

That synergy is natural, that cohesion is in the blood, and that survival and elasticity is at the core of a family's overall readiness.

FAMILY READINESS

Of course, you want to be proactive for your family. We all want what's best for them. If we can prepare and anticipate what's coming, we can be ready for it. And then adjust on the fly to ensure the ideal outcome for them. Do not wait for the Jackal to be sniffing at the door to your home, waiting for the kids to walk out into their peer pressure environment. Do not wait to address the digital Jackals lurking on the Internet, preying upon unprepared family members, and the elderly with a scam to take advantage and steal their identity or their retirement.

Family Readiness Audit
With a Family Readiness Audit you can take that first proactive step to knowing what you don't know. How attractive a target are your aging parents? Has their affluence or success made them a higher profile target?

Families need to focus on understanding their resilience. This can be accomplished informally, or formally through a **Family Readiness Audit**. Questions should be asked about what assets are important enough to warrant protection – people, their lives of course. Some property, homes, or occasionally some sentimental items may need protection. Most property can be insured, transferring the economic risk to a policy because in the end most property items are just a material thing that can be replaced. A family's personal identity, their information, and their reputation are all worth protecting. The identities of the family members and their personally identifying information (PII) are key assets that are hard to replace and are critical. Material things are different in that they can **just be purchased again** after the insurance claims are processed. **Protect what matters most.**

A family can practice its readiness with hiking and camping.

Source: Getty images

Once a family knows what it needs to protect it can undergo an assessment of what needs to be done to protect those items from specific threats to their survival. What threats and hazards exist that will reduce their ability to survive the crisis and thrive thereafter? These concerns should be prioritized by severity and likelihood.

A home defense review or Security Needs Assessment (SNA) is also critical to the family's readiness as it pertains to what technology, people, policies, procedures, systems, supplies, and resources are needed to properly ensure that the home and its contents are protected.

If the family has to shelter in place for a period of civil unrest or terrorist attack, does the family have what it needs? Does the family have enough of what it needs? Those supplies need to be in good shape, in proper quantities, and be usable even if they have been in storage for months or years.

You can understand the vulnerabilities that exist in your neighborhood and your home so that you can address these ahead of time. Is your home ready for your newborn baby? Has it been properly prepared to deal with the safety issues inherent in a modern home for a new child? Stairwells, electrical outlets, hazardous chemicals under sinks? As new parents these are typically proactively addressed and our family relationships really help in this regard. Our parents have been there, our grandparents have been there – they know and share their experience with us.

How does your neighborhood appear from a targeting perspective for crime? Is your home an easy mark for burglars or a home invasion? Has your family found itself in the middle of a city with a socio-economic bullseye for gangs or criminals? If you live in an affluent suburb, is your home arranged to allow an easy approach for teenage criminals, or a more sophisticated home invasion? A Family Readiness Audit would include a home security review, and help you make adjustments to your landscaping, your lighting, your locks and alarms, and your posture.

Family Readiness Plan

Once you have the audit completed, you can now properly spend the right amount of resources to tackle the gaps identified in your current arrangement. You might need some minor improvements to landscaping to reduce the places that people can hide around your front door or garage. Maybe an improvement in the lighting along your driveway can help you increase the natural surveillance as you approach the drive at night. Whatever is needed is put in place and the plan is written around the reality you have revealed. The plan outlines the objectives, the resources, the likely concerns, and the responses desired. It will assign roles and responsibilities. Don't forget to exercise the plan and update it regularly.

The Family Readiness Plan can really open your eyes and put in place the mitigations needed to deal with weather, crime, pandemic, civil unrest or economic collapse. Are you ready? Let's find out.

Weather

Growing up in the South we learned quickly in life that tornadoes are part of each spring and summer. We knew to watch the skies and pay attention to developing conditions because severe weather could develop quickly – bringing heavy rain, flash flooding, lightening, high winds, hail, and of course- tornadoes. Where were we to go, what was safest, and when we should move were all decisions we were exposed to from kindergarten through college.

We found ourselves on the baseball field one hot humid summer afternoon, and a quickly developing thunderstorm moved in and we all moved to the baseball dugouts to take shelter. No one had been listening to the radio, cellphone alerts didn't exist back then, and the lush tree lines obscured the horizon. Before we knew it, the skies grew dark, lightening began to strike and the air grew still. The coaches moved us to the dugout – the kids, the lightening, and aluminum bats didn't go well together. And in short order we had high winds, heavy rain, and then large hail pounding on the roof of our dugout shelter. We hadn't been there for five minutes when lightening began to strike around us.

Everyone made it through another stormy afternoon, but seeing our coaches make the call to move to the dugouts was a simple example of having a plan, having the awareness to see the weather indicators, and make a good urgent decision to move us to the nearest shelter.

Medical

Medical emergencies happen all the time. Children are particularly prone to accidents, broken bones, and skinned knees. Having a plan to deal with medical emergencies is very important when children are around. Infant and child CPR are crucial skills for families to learn, as well as having a well-stocked first aid kit along with the know-how to use it.

Paying attention to children, spouses, and aging parents when engaging in outdoor activities is key to identifying hazards like heat stroke and heat exhaustion. While organized sports provide some level of awareness from coaches, activities in the wilderness or on the water can require an additional level of preparedness to know where the urgent care will come if needed, or where you will need to go to get it promptly.

Crime

Crime is considered a form of a significant emotional event as it can lead to pain, emotional distress, anxiety, depression, and other severe results. Almost all victims experience a sense of being violated – either of their person or of their home or personal space. Depending on the severity of the criminal incident, the emotions and the anguish that are felt may be far reaching.

The National Crime Prevention Council has for years put out the public service announcement for society with McGruff the Crime Dog, and Take a Bite out of Crime. These efforts look to raise the awareness of families, neighborhoods, and children to strangers, assaults, drugs and bullies, and suspicious people in and around schools. McGruff tells us to lock our doors and windows, keep the lights on when away, and to get involved in Neighborhood Watch. Are you as a parent following McGruff's suggestions? Are you talking about Stranger Danger with your children?

What is your plan for a home invasion? What is your plan for when your child is approached by a stranger on the walk home from school? Is your spouse being targeted online by sextortion? The Jackal will use technology to his advantage. Sometimes we let them do it because we aren't paying attention. Has their email been compromised and is that email used for your online banking? Have you communicated your plans and expectations to your spouse? To your children?

Perhaps it makes sense to find some age-appropriate training for self-defense for children and spouses. They might have an interest in martial arts or taking a self-defense class that is only of their gender. Men and women have shown that they learn better in gender-specific classes among their peers that understand their reality better than their peers of the other sex.

Pandemic

Clearly pandemics are back in the headlines, as the world grapples with COVID-19 and its mutations. How was your family prepared for the occupational, economic, and restrictive nature of what occurred in the recent months?

Some families are thriving in the stay-at-home environment, their mindsets adjusted promptly, and their jobs are safe in a virtual environment. Other families have struggled with the illness, dealt with aging parents in a compromised state or nursing home, or lost their job.

Families need to apply all five of the pillars of resilience to get through such a wide ranging, and highly impactful disaster as a pandemic. They will need a sense of reality, awareness, fitness, a survival mindset, skills, and relationships to get through a second wave.

Civil Unrest

What we have also seen is the development of civil unrest in urban areas around a secondary event of police actions resulting in an undesired and unnecessary death. Police brutality, racial injustice and social-economic distress are fueling civil unrest in the U.S. of late. Is your family geographically centered in a bullseye of unrest? Or are you operating in a completely isolated, perhaps sheltered environment in a suburb or affluent gated community?

Some affluent families and private family offices are finding themselves in neighborhoods that have never seen violence or unrest. They are rightly questioning their readiness to deal with protests that turn violent. What is your family plan when this Jackal arrives and your spouse or children are home without you? Perhaps one demonstrates better common sense and decides it's time to get out of town until things cool down.

Do you have a safe haven in your home? Better to make the smart decision, than freeze in place and allow this situation to unravel in a few short minutes on your doorstep.

Lack of Electricity and Water

A lack of electricity is at the core of true economic collapse as so many facets of our modern lives rely on electricity. In the 80s and most of the 90s radio and television were the primary means of communication. Now, in our digitally and wirelessly connected world – we rely heavily on networks of data, over cellular lines, fiber, satellite, home "cable tv" systems, and business Internet networks.

Gas station pumps, water utilities, heating and air, hospital machinery, lighting, and manufacturing will all stop without power. If a family is going to shelter in place, there needs to be a secondary or even tertiary source of electricity, be it manual or solar, a generator, or battery backup with a recharging capability.

Water is a primary need that will be in short supply once power goes. We rely heavily on clean water supplied directly to our homes, businesses, and factories by the utilities that require electricity.

Without clean water we will be moving towards sanitation risk and health issues, followed by dehydration and loss of life. Finding ways to ensure your family has access to power and water is critical as society struggles with keeping those utilities working.

Collapse

With several of these new scenarios developing, and their conditions ebbing and flowing across the U.S., it is important to not underestimate the potential for a broader result. The pandemic, as it synchronizes with the unrest and the massive unemployment, race-based violence, and cyber concerns is developing into a potentially catastrophic economic collapse for countries.

We have entered, experts say, into an economic downturn not seen since the Great Depression of the 1920s. Food lines are long in the urban areas, joblessness creates anxiety and increases crime. Police are not able to respond to all calls for help, and people begin to feel restless and hopeless. When certain conditions exist where key support elements of power, information, food supply, water, banking, and safety are no longer reliable we could see a collapse of society. Power, water, sanitation, and medical support will all grind to a halt during a collapse and your family must be ready.

Our society is fragile – how ready is your family to deal with a breakdown where there is no power, no clean water and no one coming to the rescue when these Jackals show up at your door in a hungry pack.

Financial Distress

Finances are the top stressor for relationships as spouses deal with priorities for saving or spending. The discussion about what kind of lifestyle the new couple will live as they form a family, have children, raise them, and progress through their lives together.

It's important to have a solid hold on your financial planning for your family. How you will deal with shortfalls of income, emergency expenses for medical or home repairs, and what will you do for college and the advancement of your children so that they can have an even better chance at life than you have had?

Wills, Estates, POAs, and Legacies

Tied directly to financial readiness are your estate plans, wills, powers-of-attorney and what will happen to the children if you pass on unexpectedly. Do not take lightly this level of dark planning. If you don't wake up in the morning, or the plane carrying you and your spouse on vacation does not make it to the destination, what will happen to your children, your home, your estate? You have a legacy, protect it.

This is not anxiety anyone needs to carry – and you have to have a grip on the reality. No one wants the state to care for their kids if they pass. No one wants their home and estate to be stuck in probate awaiting some judge to make a decision about what will happen to those assets when your children and their guardians will likely need them promptly.

Shelter in Place

One of the things we talk about with civil unrest, crime, and natural disasters is when to shelter in place and when to evacuate. This is one of the toughest decisions that families will make as disasters and adversity rear their ugly heads.

As my friends and colleagues, Jeff Kirkham and Jason Ross put it in their book, *Beginner Emergency Survival Preparedness*, do you Bug In? (shelter in place) or Bug Out? (evacuate or move to a Bug Out Location or BOL).

Courtesy of Jeff Kirkham and Jason Ross

Sheltering in place assumes you have the necessary tools, resources, and safety to stay where you are for the current conditions and for the near future. Let's say a tornado blows through your hometown and your home is spared. You may be able to stay in that home, as long as your home is safe, power and water are available, looting is controlled, and you don't need to leave the house due to a gas leak or other adjacent threat.

Perhaps you have a plan for severe weather - a place to go when the warnings were sounded – a basement, a first-floor windowless room, a reinforced area like a safe room, or storm shelter. You have supplies, backup power, home defense capabilities and supportive relationships to help you get through this misfortune. You are prepared for these events. Jason and Jeff called these "preps" and refer to those as assets you have deemed necessary to be prepared.

In your current location you have "preps" in place. In some cases, like your Go-Bag, you can bring some preps with you. And, as long as conditions do not change – you can continue to shelter in place with those existing preps. The questions arrive as conditions develop. Does your REAL Awareness allow you to track changing conditions? It should.

The same would be true for a terrorist attack in your city. It all really depends upon the nature of the attack, which way the winds may be blowing, or the direction evacuees might be fleeing. Is your home squarely in the evacuation route for a major city? Will your doorstep be the stage upon which your readiness plays out? Are you sheltering in place, and if so, will your preps allow you to stay? If you make the decision to Bug Out of the area, and evacuate with the masses you may actually be increasing the risk to your family.

Evacuation

Evacuation or the Bug Out comes when you cannot stay where you are with confidence. You have enough information to know that you will not remain safe, you will not be well resourced, and you may no longer be protected from the elements.

This is where planning is key. If you had to evacuate tonight due to civil unrest or a natural disaster, where is your family going to go? Have you established a Bug Out Location, or BOL?

How will you get there (on foot or by vehicle)? And what will you need to take with you? There are a hundred additional questions to be answered – and you should be answering those *today*, not when the Jackal decides to show his face.

Every family is different. Some have no kids, some have 10 kids, a dog, a goldfish and an aging parent, perhaps a mobility challenged spouse. You need to take into account all the aspects of the assets you intend to move from one location to another. Are their Go-Bags sufficient? Will the BOL support their arrival and sustain their stay? Do they have power? Clean water? Medical support?

And if you decide to depart, to Bug Out, how do you do it? Whether you are leaving your office for home, or your home for your bug out location, your safer location. This could be a cabin in the mountains, a relative's home outside of town, or the beach house.

It really is about tradeoffs, your plan, your preps and assessing your conditions. Your awareness will inform your decision process.

Which Bug Out Method to Use?
Which Bug Out Method is Most Critical

Bug IN at Home	Bug OUT at Car	Bug OUT in other vehicle	Bug OUT on Foot
+Keep ALL Preps	+Keep Some Preps	+Retain Few Preps	+Almost No Preps
+Familiar Place	+Fast Travel	+Faster Than Walking	+Still Barely Mobile
+Near Friends	+Some Protection	+Avoids Traffic	- No Protection
+No Travel Risk	+Warm/Clean	- No protection	- Wet/Dirty/Tired
- Near Violence?	- Traffic Jams?	- Wet/Dirty	- Very Slow
- Target for Theft	- Enough Gas?	- Enough Gas?	- Target of Violence

Courtesy of Jeff Kirkham and Jason Ross

Is your awareness based in reality? Are you "fit" enough to make the move? Check your mindset. You must be ready for a risky move across town or the state to your BOL.

Do you have the skills to move your family in a caravan across the state at night when there is little power, no law enforcement, and no 911 in case of emergency?

Are there key relationships (fellow "preppers," relatives, likeminded people) who can support your travel? Can you make some stops at key locations?

Family Readiness Practice

Families can run drills to move them to safer locations within the house, in case of tornado or fire, of course. Families can practice their fire escapes at home. Maybe you tell the younger children that you are going to "camp out" in the house, by moving everyone into your designated safe haven for a few hours.

They can also do adventure drills where the parents and kids need to grab their Go-Bags, get themselves and their pet Fluffy to the car, so the family must "get out of town" for an adventure. Make every departure for the weekend a mobilization drill. And, if your cabin in the mountains is your BOL, perhaps it's time to actually do it right. Use your "preps" and exercise them fully.

Setting the tone for practice runs for children and anxious parents can really help make exercising your plans more effective.

Shelter in Place Supplies

Your family needs to fully understand what you need to get through a typical week, with your caloric intake, your water usage, your fuel and power needs, medicines, and lastly what other outliers do you need to handle your family's unique signature of consumption. What do your pets need? What do your live-in parents consume or require for quality of life?

Make a list. Purchase the supplies. Rotate the supplies regularly.
As you cut into 15 percent of the supplies, start to replenish them
on a monthly basis. By the time you work through your cans of
beans, your bottled water, and your rice and flour, you'll have
replenished it by the end of the year.

You should really focus on staying in a safe location as long
as possible, so long as you have what you need. Shelter and
defense are hard to find once you depart your home, your
neighborhood, or your family's locations.

REAL Relationships as you consider Shelter-in-Place are critical.
There is so much value in your neighbors, and others adjacent
to your property. It is worth investing the time to get to know
everyone in your area, what skills they have, resources they may
have access to, and whether or not they are like-minded in your
resilience and readiness. (*Perhaps they've read this book too?*)

A smart conversation among like-minded neighbors may
further inform your decision to stay or go. What if you decided
to depart an area because you were missing certain skills?
Or certain medical supplies? And, all you really needed to
know was that your neighbor, two townhouses down (that
you've never spoken to except for at the mailbox) is a doctor
who has a robust first aid kit with medicine inside his home
with a saferoom. That doctor may have the skills needed to
supplement what you don't have.

The same applies to your Bug Out Location. Is this a mountain
cabin retreat timeshare that you bought and use with family
members? Do you know who else stays in the nearby cabins?
Staying a full tank of gas distance away from a major city is a
good rule of thumb if you really need to be away from people.
This is hard to do east of the Rockies, but it's possible; especially
when you take into account people will almost always only
take the path of least resistance. Finding yourself a place that is
challenging to get to on foot might reveal a good option.

Out West, your options are better for that BOL. The challenge
may be establishing your means of getting to that BOL from a

farther distance – East Coast, or further than a couple tanks of gas in your Bug Out Vehicle.

Is this BOL you've selected just undeveloped land, an hour outside of DC on the West Virginia border on which you've placed a camper-trailer from which you hunt during the fall season? Or this could be a second home, with a cabin and some modern amenities at one of the nearby ski resorts.

What about investing in a rural community or township by buying a small house there? Spend some time there in the off-season and build some relationships that matter. If a large-scale collapse happens, or if you need to spend significant time there, it'll be easier to barter, exchange labor for supplies, or similar with people with whom you already have relationships, than trying to develop rapport and trust as a cold shot, with no previous knowledge of each other.

Family "Everyday Carry" brings us to a different topic wherein you are now responsible for creating the necessary items for our family members to have with them regularly, or at least as things begin to heat up. Our awareness gives us an indication that our Go-Bags, or our Bug Out Vehicles, might be needed in the near term.

Many of us who come from law enforcement, the military, or national security are used to having with us those items that we know will be most handy if we need to make our way from office to our homes during a time of civil unrest, natural disaster, etc. We have discussed this in our Personal Resiliency section. The same must apply to each of our family members, and those items should be adjusted based on age, maturity, ability to carry a load, and perhaps reliability.

Backpacks are the best for Go-Bags and, as we mentioned before, they should include core items such as nutrition bars, a tourniquet and first aid items, a multi-tool, water, and maybe a firearm and ammunition for those who are trained and licensed. Depending on your environment, your job, your location, and the threat environment you are most likely to find yourself in every day, you may want to consider what constitutes your "Everyday Carry" items.

In your family, you may have a newborn, where diapers and formula are key to your daily "survival." Perhaps an elderly parent is in a wheelchair, and some minimal tools and spares might be needed to ensure that that apparatus remains operational as long as possible. Perhaps oxygen is needed for someone in your family, or insulin for diabetes. And what must come with insulin is an ability to keep it refrigerated.

There are a lot of things to think about in "Everyday Carry" for a family. It's best to brew a good cup of coffee on a relaxing Saturday morning and just start writing. Keep the list with you as you move through your day, things will come to mind. Then as you reflect on the weekend on a Sunday night – recap what your activities were, what items you might need, and put them on the shopping list. Once you've handled the weekend, try it on a couple different weekdays – and see if anything more gets added to your list after you consider the workweek. You'll find you'll capture most of the things you need.

Go-Bags for Everyone

In Chapter 10, we discussed Personal Resiliency and listed out the core items for a Go-Bag for an individual. Think of that list as what a normal adult should have in their kit. When you build out Go-Bags for the family, you can take into account sharing the load for kids, and spreading that weight across several people.

As you step through each of your family member's "Everyday Carry" list, you can also add to that the concepts of location, daily activities, and mobility. Are your kids riding the bus to school? How will they be retrieved if an incident requires them to find their way home because the buses are not running?

You need to step through – and perhaps write down – the various angles of how your family will operate, where your children are during the day, what might need to be in their kit that isn't in

yours. More importantly - what things can you leave out because they are, after all, kids? Much of this is common sense.

Remember you can do adventure test runs with whatever you come up for Go-Bags for them. See how those bags work for the kids – are they fitting well? Could they actually walk a couple miles with that weight? And in the end – would they actually use the items you put in there? Or know how to do so?

You have to practice and exercise whatever Go-Bag you have built, whatever "Everyday Carry" item you have added, and the bigger plan to Bug Out, on foot or by vehicle to your location of choice.

Vehicles

Vehicle preparedness is not to be overlooked here. You should always keep your vehicle fueled with at least half a tank of gas, basic tools, some food and water, a first aid kit, foul weather gear, and jumper cables.

Keeping the vehicle properly maintained is a must. Today's vehicles, while very reliable, do have an inherent plethora of electronics that can, and do, go bad. Sometimes unexpectedly, and in some cases, catastrophically. Some vehicles are naturally resistant to certain kinds of threats, an electro-magnetic pulse (EMP) for example – typically created from the detonation of a nuclear weapon – will fry most electronics In most vehicles. But the older the vehicle, the less dependent it is on vulnerable technology, and more reliant it can be on "analog" mechanical systems – ignition, distribution, fuel and water pumps, etc.

This aspect of mobility is key and while we won't go into detail, Red Five's REAL Skills includes modules on vehicle selection, load out, navigation, operation – both on- and off-road.

What's in the Cars

Totes and dedicated vehicle bags are good ways to aggregate what would be considered "family" or team gear that should be in the car, or in a location where it's easy to throw right into the trunk, and go.

For the well-prepared, Ken Cameron of Cameron Advanced Mobility has provided the following list as a good place to start for items in the vehicle that will be used to Bug Out:

Gloves with dexterity
Recovery sling (used as tree saver)
Recovery strap (used for recovering vehicles or towing)
Pulley block (used with winch for recovery and potentially moving objects)
3/8" x 10' chain for abrasive environments
Hi-lift type jack
2 stage bottle jack
4-8 traction aids (aluminum or plastic flotation traction aids)
Shovel
Pic axe
12 volt receiver plugs
USB for charging multiple devices
Small 12 volts compressor (ViAir)
Tire patches or tube
Valve stem removal tube with spare valve cores
Small axe/hatchet
Machete (depending on location)
SAE, and metric wrenches and sockets (1/4" to 1 ¼"; 8mm-24mm)
Channel locks pliers (3 sizes)
Needle nose pliers
Lineman pliers
Snap ring pliers
Flat head screwdriver
Phillips head screwdriver (different sizes)
Pry bars (one 24"; one 12")
Assorted hammers
Hex head and Torx head tools
Large crescent wrench (3")
Razor blade knife
Chisels
Multimeter
Test light
Assorted connections
Electrical wire (various gauges, 1 roll of proper gauges)
Electrical tape (4 rolls)
Hi pressure tape (4 rolls)
Fuses and relays (vehicle specific)
Di-electric grease for wet connections (1 tube)
High strength glue (epoxy)
JB weld (small tubes)
Silicone (tube)
Water weld (to fix cooling components)
WD40 (large can for lubrication and water displacement)
550 cord (200')
Ratchet straps, cam straps for lashing (2 of each)
500' rope (manilla or nylon)
Water jugs, 10 gallons
Water purifier
Water siphon for transferring

For those outfitting their vehicles for situations that could require additional supplies, here are items to include for load-out.

Headlamps
Batteries
Multi-tool
GPS
Maps
Watches
Short Wave Radio
FMRS Radios (2 or more)
Toilet wipes, Toilet Paper
Soap
N95 Masks
Gas Masks
Lip Balm
Feminine Hygiene
Caffeine Tablets
MREs (Meals Ready to Eat)
Dehydrated meals – your brand of choice, high quality (4 days)
Emergency Rations (2,000 calories per family member)
Ground Coffee or Instant Creamer
Spoons, Forks, Plates, Cups
Paper Towels
Sleeping Bags
Sleeping Pads
Gore-Tex (or similar) Jackets
Fleeces/Layered for warmth
Outdoor Pants
Thermal Underwear (cold weather)

Socks
Beanie Hats
Boots (broken in)
Leather Belt
Sunglasses
Family Tent
Camouflage Cover for Tent
Spare Tire
Heavy rifle
Rifle ammunition
Rifle magazines
Rifle sling
Chest rig for magazines
Handgun
Handgun holster
Handgun magazines
Handgun ammunition
Handgun magazine pouch
Flashlight
Binoculars
Lighters
Matches
First Aid Kit (trauma)
Camp Stove
Camp Stove Fuel
Pot Grabber
Folding Knife
Fixed Blade Knife
Knife Sharpener
Axe Sharpening Puck
Collapsible Saw

As you strive to be REAL about your family readiness: Follow the 5 pillars.

- Do a Family Readiness Audit
- Write your Family Readiness Plan, tailored to your conditions
- Build your Go-Bags, specific to each family member, and share the load
- Have a plan to shelter-in-place or evacuate
- Prep the vehicle(s)
- Do a practice run to the Bug Out Location

BUSINESS ADVERSITY

Business Adversity can present itself in many ways – shortage of cash, decreased demand for your services, natural disaster, heavy competition in your industry, obsolescence of your technology or services, litigation, poor management, or any combination of the above. It is critical that you are ready for the Jackals that are zeroing in on your livelihood.

If you are working in an industry that has been around for less than a couple years you may want to begin monitoring the health of the industry for your relevance. You should be paying attention every day to your livelihood – but when your industry is new, many challenges are apparent, and the changes can be fast.

Try starting with a **Business Preparedness Audit**. There are a number of key areas you should be paying attention to as your company develops, matures, and moves through its life cycle – startup, to adolescent and growing, to maturity in your industry. Take the time to run through this process, or better yet, have an outsider do this with a fresh look on things, apart from your perceptions, preconceived notions, or blindness to obvious shortcomings.

Start-ups and Cash

The importance of cash can be even more crucial if you are the owner of a start-up, a version of business that is cash-intensive and capital is king. Do you have enough cash to survive a pandemic? How have these past few months gone for you and your team?

Be prepared for a cyber-attack or data breach that calls into question your ability to protect your clients' privacy, or their identifying information. Small businesses are often the target, especially early on their life cycle, as investors don't want to spend the money on infrastructure and security. It's about grabbing market share, getting to profitability, and locking in intellectual property that matter.

In talking with various wealth managers, investment houses and understanding how they view risk, both physical and digital, it is clear that mitigation efforts against catastrophic or even medium risks are not well executed nor funded. It's not what they want to hear. They are driving to the dollar. However, if you are an entrepreneur that has bootstrapped the company, running with no debt, lean margins, and a promising future – it might be well worth your time to protect that sweat equity that no one can replace. Investors care about their money, but they won't care about your start-up.

So as you are determining how to spend your capital on the front end – it's a good idea to think about analyzing the risks to your capital, your data, your assets – so that as the captain of your startup you know what will sink your ship to the bottom of the ocean, not just what might slow down the profit in troubled waters.

Sourcing Talent

Another critical area that is neglected and often becomes the focus of adversity for business is poor hiring practices and retention of talent. **You need to hire resilient people, or at least people who have resilient traits.** Across the board in business it's important to exercise discipline in hiring, not just the pace, but the quality and the spend.

I've worked hard over the years to figure out the best way to find, and source talent. It is, without question, the single hardest thing to do when running your own business. Quality talent that wants to help you grow is not easy to come by. I'm sure professional recruiters would argue that they make it easy. My experience with recruiters is that, while they offer a simple approach, they typically find whoever is available and try to sell them back into your firm. On the other hand, the concept of poaching really good talent from another competitor is much more difficult, but can pay off. There are some really good recruiters, headhunters and executive search firms out there – no doubt; and I applaud their efforts in a tough task.

But, know that if you do it wrong, follow poor guidance, select poorly, screen lackadaisically, or hire too quickly – you will feel the pain. Trust me.

Follow these tips to hiring the right talent:

1. Be clear on your needs – what gets you to the next level may not be what has gotten you to your current level of success. Start with the end in mind, even if it is an interim step to your ultimate goal.

2. Know that you can set these "milestones" in your business; no one is going to tell you what's normal.

3. Once you know what you need, get help on current trends for job descriptions and places to find talent. Understand where you are fishing for talent, and is it the right pond for those fish?

4. Once you start getting resumes and candidates, screen them well. Get more than three – and set a means of assessing them. Equal process is better, that way you are comparing apples to apples, etc.

5. If time allows, run a probationary period as a 1099 or a temporary employee. This doesn't usually work for

executives – but the more you can get in a test run the better.

6. Follow the legal and compliance issues around your hires. Don't lose a good one because you took a short-cut on the process and created a problem that didn't need to arise.

7. Do background checks, and not just through some "internet service." Hire a firm that knows how to do background investigations. The higher the position within your company – the more scrutiny these candidates need to meet your threshold of excellence.

8. Let a trusted lieutenant do the first round of interviews, and give them some really hard questions to ask. Make sure you have them write down the answers given.

9. Make sure you are hiring for culture. As your company grows, it might seem easy to find people, but you'll notice that they don't fit your culture. Sometimes this isn't discovered until they are deep inside your operation and rocking the boat.

10. Put eyes on them, meet them, have a meal, and really poke around the professional issues that came out of the first interview. If you find an inconsistency – dig. People are well-trained in "resume writing" and "interviewing." And not as many are well trained in interviewing and "interrogating." How important is your business? How willing are you to keep a problem employee out of your leadership or management team?

Growth Plateaus

Businesses will go through a life-cycle, and if you are fortunate to find yourself in growth mode you will find yourself hitting plateaus. These plateaus can come as client demand shifts; or as competition in your sector increases.

Don't let a slowdown, or a plateau in your revenue stop you from achieving your goals. You will need to be aware that a plateau is happening. You will need to watch the numbers and assess where you are in the cycle. Listen to clients as they tell you what they want – don't tune them out.

When these plateaus hit, get your team together and analyze it. What's happening in your market? Have you priced yourself out of the running, or are clients just getting more cost conscious? Ask some hard questions of your middle management. Call your clients – if your communication methods have slid from personal to impersonal that's a problem. Get your communication on track. Talk to your clients, meet with them, and get down to brass tacks. No one likes to give bad news, but you need to ask for it. Thank them for it. Same goes for your vendors – be honest with them. Clarity in communication when these challenges arise is critical.

Litigation

My father has run his own engineering and construction businesses for decades. He says if you haven't been threatened with a lawsuit or actually been sued then you haven't really been running your business all-out. There are people out there who use their attorneys as their first line of defense. When expectations aren't managed, when contracts are unclear, when deliverables are soft, and especially when politicians begin to see themselves at risk for the existing relationship – it's time to start looking around for the attorneys. The sharks will line up and you have to be ready for a street fight.

"
> "One great piece of advice I received early on is do not go cheap with accountants or attorneys. When it goes bad in either finance or legal, you want really good people in your corner. That has paid off time and again."
>
> — Kris Coleman
"

Those of you who think the world is all about negotiation, people doing the right thing, following the rules, and following due process – you are in for a rude awakening. **Sometimes the Jackal gets the first shot and you are not ready for it.**

General James Mattis (USMC Retired) said, "Be polite, be professional, but have a plan for killing everybody you meet." You can apply this concept to potential litigation, fierce competition, or difficult negotiations.

Be polite, be professional, do the job well, over-deliver, on time and within budget – but be prepared to be sued for absolutely no reason. Find the balance, ride the line – you'll sleep better.

Competition

Competition is really about the leadership of your company or your livelihood, and whether or not you and your firm want to maintain relevance. You can start out running fast, you can opt to not innovate and keep doing that for a while, but at some point you will have to innovate to keep up with the competition. And this does not apply only to tech-industry firms. It applies across the board, internal processes and external deliverables and service offerings – the reason is that your supply chain for talent, for raw materials, for client acquisition is going to change. It will if it hasn't already since you started reading this book. Innovate or die, I say.

Calling It – When to Start Over

I'm not a fan of quitting anything. I would say however that you need to know when the time has come to "call it" – either as a company, as a service line, or with a client. I have been fortunate to not have to file bankruptcy, or to sell. We have managed our debt smartly, conservatively, and kept our costs under control while we watched the revenue stream with a careful, but optimistic eye.

What I have done – had to do – was fire bad clients, regardless of their value, gross revenue opportunity, or relationship. Going beyond the line is dangerous for you, your reputation, and your company. It is painful, but this option is absolutely a luxury for sole proprietors, founders and majority shareholders.

Sometimes a client comes in with demands, unfounded, forced upon them by others, or just because they think they can take advantage of you. They are pushing you – hard charging people will do that. They will see how far you will go for the dollar. In two different instances I've walked away from big clients. In the end, those demands placed on us would have hurt the company, had a negative impact on my employees, or created massive operational, litigation, or reputational risk that just wasn't worth it. I called it. Sometimes you have to do it.

Be sure to communicate well to all those key stakeholders – your board, your shareholders, your leadership and management teams, and your employees. Be transparent enough – they don't likely need to know the dirty details, but in the end – give them what they need to know, so they have confidence that you are making the right decision. And if you can't figure that out – maybe you need to reassess.

In those instances, you must have a plan to recover, you must have a plan to cut costs and re-tool to keep the business going. So – never just call it on a hunch. Think about all that you've just read. I'm suggesting you:

- [ ] Be aware of the options. Base "your call" on reality, not fantasy.
- [ ] Be fiscally and emotionally fit to handle it. Look at it clinically and from different angles.
- [ ] Apply a survival mindset.
- [ ] Apply your legal, financial, negotiation skills; and
- [ ] Use your relationships to think it through-advisors or mentors. Take the emotion out of it.

Do these look familiar? They should – they are again, the 5 Pillars of Resilience – only this time in the business paradigm.

Watch your cash position closely.

Hire for resilience.

Be ready for battle.

Communicate clearly, during good and bad times.
Get your business set for your REALity. It's up to you, the leader, to do this for your livelihood, your team, your business.

LEADERS INSTILL
BUSINESS PREPAREDNESS

Business Preparedness is all about the leadership. You - the leader, the founder, the boss. Whether you are a minority-owned government contractor, a CEO of a woman-owned corporation, or the founder of a startup, you have to set the tone for resilience, readiness, and preparedness.

We have talked about how our entire process – the 5-3-1 System – is set in the foundation of the individual. If the individuals are resilient then their families and their businesses will follow. They must be resilient in order to achieve the 1 goal – survive and thrive.

This is never more true than in startups and single member LLCs, sole proprietors on the growth plan, and groups looking to drive into a long healthy lifecycle. If the leader is a clueless visionary – not giving resiliency a second thought beyond his golden parachute – then the company will be heavily reliant on the second in command to establish the plan for preparedness and contingencies.

This is common in companies where the founder is a dreamer and innovator, smart enough to bring aboard an integrator as a number two to really handle the business operations. Those companies typically do well, with that kind of synergy at the top.

For those that don't get that benefit of a strong COO or Managing Partner to execute the vision of the founder, those companies struggle as they are not based in reality – but in the fantasy hopes of someone not thinking about other external forces that are looming, the Jackals in the shadows.

Culture Matters

Many times, in business preparedness and readiness, it comes down to culture. As companies grow and evolve, they will take on a culture. Corporate culture is a thing that has become a well-studied subject by top business schools, leadership programs, and talent professionals. Establishing a strong culture will help companies survive tough times, especially if the culture includes concepts such as resilience and preparedness.

If the culture is all about devil-may-care office rules, open keg parties, ping pong tables in the break room, and no real rigor, then you may be facing some challenges if things take a turn for the worse. Is that population really ready for a tough time of economic pressure?

Some of those trends we saw in the 2000's and 2010's aren't all bad. Working from home and progressive approaches to the use of video and virtual technology have both proven to be critical business processes and methods to put in use when the COVID-19 pandemic arrived on our shores in early 2020.

The culture can have all those luxurious comforts and benefits but it doesn't have to ignore the key concepts for business preparedness. Culture needs to be figured out, nurtured, developed, and reinforced when it's right.

Leaders can setup company activities that reinforce resilient behaviors – scavenger hunts for key preparedness equipment; hiking or outdoor activities; fitness challenges; establishing satellite communications during long distance activities; developing Go-Bags for all your employees as a brown bag lunch event; philanthropic events for local charities that help during natural disasters; competitions to see which team survives; and, encouraging outside projects and reading that support the five pillars of resilience – awareness, mindset, fitness, skills, and relationships.

Understanding SWOT

As we talk about business – we have to keep our **REAL Awareness** high. One of the ways many executives maintain their awareness is to create dashboards that help them understand their business processes, and where they are at any given time. At Red Five we followed a process setup by the Ford Motor Company called the Business Process Review (BPR) where we look at all projects and business processes weekly to make sure we are on track. My managers provide a stoplight assessment each time we meet to understand where they are, either on their project or with their internal assessment of finance, recruiting, or contracts. A simple red, yellow, or green gives the leadership a snapshot of health each week – and employees are encouraged to jump in and call it like it is. This keeps things based in reality, and not biased based on someone's career, the fact that they are having a bad quarter, or that the client is an asshole. Again – that stuff happens.

A big part of the BPR and of any leadership meetings that occur must be an understanding of SWOT, that is: strengths, weaknesses, opportunities and threats to any business. SWOT analysis is typically portrayed in a chart. This helps flag for management and leadership key elements in each of those areas that have either already manifested, or are developing in the near-term. This is critical to a leader's awareness around the business.

REAL Awareness fits squarely in this area as you get a really good understanding of your reality by addressing SWOT and BPR. You do not want to be in a position of learning something at the end of a fiscal quarter that was going the wrong way, when you could have learned about it real-time and fixed it, avoiding the losses of profit and time that would have come with the delay in your awareness.

102

Hiring for Resilience

Culture is about the people who have been hired, their beliefs, their geography, their service mindset, and what they do. Ideally you are hiring for resilience and preparedness. Hiring for resilience is not hard; insert some scenarios about adversity into your interview process.

Be sure to pay attention to the stories that your candidates tell about their roles in those challenges. Were they proponents and supportive to a war-time CEO in a corporate fight for their lives? Were they judgmental and lacking in understanding of the challenges in running a business?

As has been discussed in the past, hiring veterans, former law enforcement, and intelligence personnel goes a long way to building in resilience into your team. Those professions, along with first responders and other high-pressure jobs, force personnel to understand processes to continue operations, even in the case of adversity or while under attack in a war zone. Mission-focused personnel help you build the culture of preparedness.

This speaks squarely to the concept of **REAL Mindset**. Hire for mindset and culture. If you are getting good people, your team will be resilient, ready and prepared. The mindset needed to persevere when the business Jackals are lurking in the shadows. The more resilient people you have with the right mindset, the better chance you will have to see one of those Jackals; whether as an insider threat on your team, or approaching from the outside, looking to take advantage of what they think is a vulnerability. The more eyes you have on your management team that can see Jackals for what they are, the better off you will be in business.

Processes

Right alongside the BPR and the use of a SWOT analysis are other key processes inside a company. As we have mentioned before – cash is king in business – and you need it to survive. It is critical for you to have eyes on processes and make sure that they are optimally established to help the company thrive. This is not about creating obstacles for maximum rigor and transparency – if you want to kill your company by making it operate like the government, that's a choice – but not a good one.

Create enough rigor, process and transparency for the size of your company. If it's just you – as a sole proprietor – keep it lean, and run it fast. You already have all the info at your fingertips. But, as the company grows you will need more processes to handle accounting, marketing, sales, project management, and contracts. Add them as you need them.

If your company is really agile and fit, you probably have a good read on it's **REAL Fitness**. How is your cash position? Cash flow? What does your utilization of labor look like? Hopefully you are running profitably, with just enough process, good revenue, low costs, and ideally paying attention to where the next process will be needed.

Business Contingencies and Plans

When it comes to **REAL Skills** in business, it's about how to navigate the minefields that are placed in front of you, the Jackals that are maneuvering, as attorneys, and competitors that are trying to steal your secrets, your clients, and your livelihood.

You have to have strong talent on your team, but they also have to be prepared with operational protections in place, emergency plans and continuity of operations planning. They need to be on the same sheet with the leadership – which goes back to your leadership, hiring, and culture.

Do not underestimate what's needed when things go bad in the business world. A natural disaster far away across the globe could impact your supply chain. A smart CEO will have alternatives in place so that her team can continue to make their products with only the smallest of hiccups in their process. Their clients will be kept happy, shareholders pleased with their resilience, and the employee bonus pool kept intact. A good risk assessment will help inform a company as to what skills they need, what resources are required and identify key processes to put in place.

"

"Conducting a risk assessment, taking stock of your situation and employing expertise to mitigate the risk will help to keep the Jackals out and retain your productive employees. The biggest issue is hiring a professional to do the risk assessment that has a methodology, and stands behind their recommendations."

—Kris Coleman

"

The risk assessment should address the assets you are protecting (e.g., people, information, reputation, etc.) and the likely threats against those assets (e.g., criminal, terrorism, civil unrest, natural disasters, etc.). The process should address the vulnerabilities of the facility and assets as well as the prioritized mitigations for those vulnerabilities - at the property line, at the hardline of the structure (walls, doors, windows), and interior considerations (saferooms, escape considerations). Lastly, risk must be calculated in a way that makes sense, highlights the benefits, and discusses what residual risk might remain after implementing the upgrades.

Standard operating procedures and a good policy might be a hedge against frivolous litigation. If you have a procedure and a policy, and people are trained and aware of them, it is harder for rogue employees to take advantage.

In addition to a good physical review, the risk assessment should address digital security and privacy issues for the facility, the business and key personnel. It isn't all about the physical, so be sure to address information technology defense as well as offensive, threat hunting cyber capabilities. The Jackals are in our systems and devices everyday – attacking relentlessly. We must be vigilant. While we want to keep them out, we have to hunt them inside our digital networks to keep them from taking advantage. A well-considered risk assessment will also help you make trade off decisions about budget versus return on investment for any particular technologies or physical upgrades. It should address the most likely threats, and consider the paths that the Jackals will most likely take to attack your people, your information and your reputation. If you have a good risk assessment, you and your business will be well-informed about how best to invest in your security and resilience. You can make tradeoffs about your risk as it pertains to insurance policies, emergency plans, work from home, travel issues, insider threats, etc.

❝

"Do not measure risks by the tools that are familiar to you, but measure risk from a holistic assessment of the evidence and then select the tools most appropriate to the situation."

—Alexander H. Hay PhD CEng PEng FICE CRM RSES, Principal, Southern Harbour Ltd, Author of After the Flood

❞

At a minimum, you must control access. Let's face it, the best way to keep a Jackal out of your office space is to never let them in in the first place. You should always maintain control (if your business allows) of who can enter your business. This is particularly true with office space and stand-alone facilities, but it will not likely work for retail. Disgruntled employees or clients, criminals or others can enter your space unless it's controlled. Active threat situations are on the rise in the U.S. and it's important to take steps to prevent their access. For retail stores, key elements will include robust and early customer interaction, good visual surveillance of all aspects of the site, and perhaps an external store "greeter," who has been trained in detecting criminal behavior. And, as always, a uniformed, armed guard can help with deterrence when other aspects of security are not providing you the results you need.

The risk assessment should drive the need for a robust **Continuity of Operations Plan (COOP)** or Business Continuity Plan. For example, a resilient company in San Francisco should have a COOP in place to deal with earthquakes and wildfires. Both of those natural phenomena have taken place in the past two decades, and now we have experienced an economic and national health calamity to add to those. Your business geography will have an impact as specific risks to specific areas matter.

Keeping enough cash on hand to weather the storm is also another key factor as touched on with startups and small businesses. Capital is critical; but that doesn't mean that cash isn't important to larger enterprises. Cash becomes even more important when revenues drop and talent must be retained, or raw materials must keep flowing. If not cash, access to capital – either through traditional banking, investors, or venture capital – must be maintained.

Technology is another key element of COOP. When the pandemic hit in early 2020, Red Five pulled its COOP off the shelf and exercised it. We had written it years prior, as we were doing more and more business in San Francisco, and we wanted our clients and employees there to know we were serious about the long view - being resilient and smart about their well-being.

When we exercised the COOP, we learned that there were a handful of key documents that were in hard copy, in safes inside the office in Virginia. We adjusted so we could access those digitally, made some minor improvements to our technology stack (already mostly in the cloud), and were able to roll into virtual work mode within two weeks.

> We regularly consult with clients about emergency plans, standard operating procedures, and various contingency plans. It's a good thing that we practice what we preach.

Emergency Action Plans (EAP) can help you handle the tactical emergency – the fire, the tornado, the earthquake and the hurricane. EAPs are also important to dealing with those malicious actors – the active shooters, the bomb threats and the cyber-attacks. This again is not a plan that sits on a shelf. It's a document that is assigned to a leader or manager whose responsibility it is to keep it current, update it based on intelligence and exercise it as needed to ensure it will actually work with existing technology, in that geography, and when combinations of threats present themselves. Jackals rarely arrive solo – they always show up in a pack.

We strongly recommend having an EAP in place for your personnel, at each location, and one that is tailored to the most likely risks at each site. Your EAP and COOP should address each of these issues:

1. Weather
2. Cyber breach
3. Terrorism
4. Civil Unrest
5. Pandemic
6. Supply Chain Disruption
7. Economic Collapse
8. The People Required
9. Shelter in Place
10. Evacuation Plan
11. Recovery Plan

We did our own risk assessment, put into play our COOP, employed the technology to execute it and have a population trained to use that technology. We had the **REAL Skills** needed to get on with our business during the pandemic.

As we know, the fifth pillar for business preparedness is relationships. We need to sow the seeds for complementary, supportive, industry and peer-based relationships to help our **REAL Relationships** for business.

Most industries have associations or councils that provide best practices, advice and guidance for companies operating in that vertical. For those who have founded their companies, these may not be your first stop for advice – but do not ignore them. As much as they may seem out of touch with your special circumstances as an entrepreneur – you will likely find helpful information there. Not all of it will be a fit, but if you walk away with one nugget of wisdom, it was worth it.

College and university alumni associations, entrepreneur support groups and professional retiree societies can help with finding talent, capital and advice when it matters most. I've called on all three of these in the past decade-plus to help with marketing, hiring, vetting of clients, etc. For me, the Society of

External Resource Organizations

- Society of Former Special Agents of the FBI
- FBI Agents Association
- Association of Former Intelligence Officers
- The American Society of Industrial Security (ASIS)

Former Special Agents of the FBI, FBI Agents Association and the Association of Former Intelligence Officers provided a great source of mentorship, advice and direction from time to time. The American Society of Industrial Security (ASIS) is another professional group in the industry that has provided some good fundamental resources as my career progressed, and I ventured out on my own.

Another key group to get involved with is a peer group, for founders, entrepreneurs and CEOs. I've been in three of these groups over the years. Each provided help and advice, and several in a "tough love" fashion with your peers providing critical reviews of your finances, your business decisions, talent selections, organizational strategies, etc. They are a compassionate ear and a critical eye for you and your livelihood and are well worth your time. I've enjoyed my association with the friends I made when I was a Vistage member, a well-known CEO peer group. I continue to benefit from those relationships I built while involved with them. They called me out on things

I wasn't ready to see or realize, as I had been too close to the topic, skewed in my perception of reality, (or just being bullheaded).

Nurture and reinforce strong cultural ties inside the company.

Do regular SWOT charts, understanding your strengths, weaknesses, opportunities, and threats.

Conduct a risk assessment to help you anticipate challenges in your near future.

Create and exercise Emergency Action Plans.

Have a Continuity of Operations Plan or Business Continuity Plan that is ready to go.

Find and foster strong, supportive peer relationships.

REAL AWARENESS

As we stated before, **REAL Awareness** is the ability to notice, put in context and realistically digest what is going on around you. That includes the physical as well as your current emotional and psychological state. If you don't have awareness of yourself, it is impossible to understand the reality around you and how it relates to the decisions, plans and actions you must take to successfully react to actions being taken against you, or developments that are not in your best family or business interests.

Many people walk around in the world today completely oblivious to how what they are doing in the moment might be affecting those around them. We run into people every day, who are blocking the aisle in the grocery store, staring at the ingredients on a can of beans, completely unaware that ten people with carts are patiently (or impatiently) waiting for them to move their cart out of the way. Same can be said of those who are staring at their phones while driving even though they should be focused on the road ahead.

Awareness takes on a new form when swimming in the ocean, traveling in a dangerous part of town, or even traveling in a country that is new to you. Culture, diseases, criminals, traffic and weather can all be very different – and one's lack of awareness of the differences from their normal geography could be fatal. A friend goes snorkeling in the ocean to relax and enjoy the wildlife, but she is smart enough and aware enough to know that with those beautiful fish come predators – some of whom might just mistake a swimmer for lunch. She makes the decision to be more aware of her environment. She knows she is in a non-typical environment with a higher risk factor.

Rick Hanson, a clinical psychologist and author of the 2018 book, "Resilient," spoke with *The Wall Street Journal* about how we can build our resilience in challenging times. Dr. Hanson, a senior fellow at the Greater Good Science Center at the University of California, Berkeley, draws on neuroscience, psychology, and mindfulness training in his work. First, find your footing. In other words, in any kind of shaky situation, you want to slow down, listen to the experts, find out what's really going on. Then, make a plan and work your plan. When you are dealing with massive uncertainty on a large scale, at least be certain about your plan for today.

When I traveled overseas for the government, we received significant modules of training to help us increase our awareness for our personal security, and for those we were assigned to protect. We were taught to identify developing scenarios that represented threats. Situational awareness, pre-attack indicators, and attack recognition skills came with the territory – whether it was Bosnia, the Middle East, Colombia, or Africa.

We had to change our thinking to adapt safely to the new environment. In doing so, we were better armed to see the world differently, and be ready for these new behaviors of those around us.

We were taught how to raise our awareness when certain indicators presented themselves. It was critical to be attuned to your environment, your local handlers, your driver, your hotel staff – so that you would not be caught off guard when the Jackal arrived.

Awareness ranged from how to handle yourself as you got on the plane headed for a foreign land, proceeding through customs in South America, to what floor your hotel room was on (will the fire truck ladders reach that floor?) How many different escape routes there were in the restaurant where you were eating dinner in Jakarta? Once on the ground, we began to assess very quickly the suspicious actions of others that might have an effect on our personal safety and, of course, the mission. Personal safety awareness is critical in today's world, in the U.S., and elsewhere in the world.

Our bodies play an important role in resilience and readiness. As we are put into different situations, we begin to see changes in our heart rate, our senses heightening. The hair may stand on the back of your neck when danger presents itself. It's important to pay attention to your senses and your gut instinct when fear or danger appear in your surroundings. If we follow some simple guidelines as we move through our lives, we can influence how our body reacts to stressors. It's fight, flight, or freeze in place.

At a certain level of awareness our body has a baseline of ability to respond, the floor of biophysical response. We typically operate above that level moving through our day. Our ability to respond may ebb and flow with our biorhythms and our state of caffeination, sleep patterns, etc. As stressors present themselves our biophysical response will drop until we have a chance to get our hands around it, develop our response, and react. This typically occurs in just a few seconds when events are critical and fast moving. During more acute, long-term crises, we may find ourselves moving through stages more slowly – a terminal illness, a bankruptcy, grieving the loss of a loved one or a major job change.

Ideally as conditions change, we go from when we wake up, relaxed and unaware, to learning about the morning news, the commute, how our family slept last night – a more informed status. Once we get into the car we may be in more danger than the remainder of our day – lots of distracted people moving in multi-ton vehicles, at high speeds, in close proximity (what could go wrong?). We should be increasing our awareness as we move through the day – understanding we are going from our commute and into a high-stress office meeting with high stakes. Is our performance being assessed? Meanwhile, children may be moving from the classroom to the playground, where bullying may be taking place. Is your child ready for that stressor? Your son or daughter should have a heightened level of awareness in that new environment. As we wrap up our day and head home, our state of awareness should continue, but it's difficult as we now have a whole day's worth of stress and stimuli to deal with, and time to think about it, distractedly during the drive home.

Maintain your REAL Awareness. There are warning signs.

Source: Red Five

This is an important concept because when the Jackal arrives with a vengeance in a physical attack, all of those biophysical responses happen in a very short time frame. You and your spouse are walking out of the movie theater and as you approach your car in the distant parking lot, you see the person in a hoodie approaching, and a gun is presented to your face. This happens very quickly . . . and the question is how do you respond? What is your body doing? It is dumping adrenaline into your system. Will your body drop below the floor of biophysical response? If so – you may just freeze in place, not knowing what to say or do. This is what people refer to when they say they were paralyzed with fear. Your mind and your muscles are unable to move because of the significant change in blood chemistry. You are not inoculated for this stress . . . the

Jackal has the advantage, and 9 times out of 10, the Jackal wins when he has the element of surprise. In order to keep your body and mind sharp, so they do NOT drop below the floor and paralyze you with fear, you must train yourself in the levels of awareness for today's world.

We should be proactively moving up and down a spectrum of awareness each day of our lives. We recommend you remain aware of your current state and make decisions to increase or decrease your awareness as conditions change. To accomplish this, we frequently apply the color codes of awareness originally put forth by the late Jeff Cooper, a former U.S. Marine. These codes still stand as a valid tool today.

Awareness Color Codes

WHITE	Really unaware of what is going on around them
YELLOW	Have a healthy level of awareness
ORANGE	Have identified a specific indicator of concern, either a person or a hazard
RED	A threat has presented itself
BLACK	Have reached a point where you are frozen, possibly in shock, at the seriousness of the threat that has presented itself

The assertion is that individuals should be aware of their current color code and move up and down the spectrum as appropriate to be ahead of the Jackal.

At the lowest level of awareness people are in "White" – oblivious to what is going on around them. One of the common themes in some police depositions is, "I never saw it coming." That person was not present, not paying attention. This is typical of people who are caught completely off guard when the Jackal arrives. These are the people who are stepping into fountains because they are busy walking down the street staring at their devices.

The next level of increased awareness is "Yellow" and people in this category have a healthy level of awareness. Consider driving to work and being on a multi-lane highway, understanding the flow of traffic, and the car in front of you slows suddenly. You, already knowing that the lane to your left is open, can move smoothly and safely without dramatic inputs to steering into that lane, and avoid the stopping car. Individuals at this level have a healthy situational awareness. They are seeing people around them; they are assessing conditions casually. On a normal hot and humid summer day in the South, we knew to expect thunderstorms and maybe violent weather, so we assessed the weather each afternoon in the yellow level of awareness. As hurricane season starts, we raise awareness to yellow as alerts and reminders are broadcast to those on the Gulf and Atlantic coasts.

"Orange" means we have identified a specific indicator of concern, either a person or a hazard. You are actually seeing what's in front of you, recognizing the concern and fixing it. As wildfires begin to develop near your community your family, and neighbors start making preparations in case the wind shifts requiring a quick but orderly departure. You start to anticipate what may happen. Like in baseball or soccer, you are anticipating where the ball will go, what you will do with it if it comes to you and how the "next play" will manifest. You already have a plan, because you have been in yellow – you live in yellow in some conditions and in geographies. Yellow is not a bad place to be.

In a more urgent scenario, you leave the convenience store one evening after picking up some ice cream on the way home to your spouse. As you step into the parking lot, you are alert enough to notice two individuals approaching as you move toward your car. These individuals may or may not be a threat, but your experience tells you this "situation" is common, that people are rolled/mugged as they walk to their car at night. Your

116

senses perk up, your heartbeat increases, your body begins to prepare itself to deal with the situation. If benign, it will pass and those individuals will move on to their business. If not, you have some very quick decisions to make – and this will come down to training, what to say and do.

The "Red" color code means that a threat has presented itself. Individuals or conditions have indicated specifically that adversity is upon you. Whether it be a tornado approaching, or persons with ill intentions. The indicators are either reliable forms of information (the weather service), or direct verbal assault, their body language, the speed and direction in which they are moving, or perhaps the attack begins with the first punch. A hurricane warning has been posted and you are using your evacuation plan (because you had moved up through yellow and orange) to take action. You must be in red to successfully deal with the situation promptly. If you are in white or yellow when these actions occur, it will be very hard to recover quickly enough to defend yourself or your family. If you are seeing the indicators in yellow, and then orange, you should be raising your alert level to red. If you are in red when the Jackal arrives – then you should be prepared to deal with him, and dispatch him with contempt.

In recent years other professionals have added "Black" as a category that people may find themselves in if caught completely unaware. Black is a condition where you are frozen, possibly in shock, at the seriousness of the threat that has presented itself. At this level there is a breakdown of your mental state, and your biophysical responses to the threat can paralyze or cripple your ability to respond.

After actions of attacks on motorcades, VIPs in vehicles have found their drivers "froze" in place. They died because they were not in the appropriate level of awareness. When the Jackal stepped in front of the limousine with the AK-47, they stomped on the brakes, bringing the car to stop, and just sat there, not taking evasive action, not driving through the threat (which might be the best and fastest option.) Their body reaction dumped adrenaline and cortisol into the bloodstream which impeded the ability to make decisions and move important muscles into action. The drivers dropped into the black. Some drivers die in places, where others are successful due to proper training including stressful scenarios. While they may have been surprised, their training allowed them to recover more quickly, to get out of the kill zone. Those that lived to tell about it were able to recognize their key role as a driver, staying in yellow, assessing the developing situation, rising through the color codes as they detected concerns, and then reacting as their training allowed them – their mind and body were ready and aware.

Emotional Awareness

Much like the dangerous environments we encountered, we also found ourselves in challenging personal interactions. We received training on how to be more emotionally aware of other people – from other cultures and from a perspective of working with them. In the government, we were trained to assess people for their vulnerabilities and proclivities, identifying what might be motivations to get them to help our country in its national security activities. We worked hard to understand individuals, to ascertain their intent, collecting small pieces of the puzzle. In law enforcement, we were trained to understand the criminal mind, why they committed those acts, and apply the techniques to investigate those people, interview those around them, and interrogate, if necessary, those involved. Eventually, our goal would be to testify in support of the cases we worked. Culture plays a huge part in awareness – knowing what personal behaviors were normal, which were offensive, what are the correct greetings and salutations in distinct instances of social behavior. Our awareness can be the absolute most important tool to getting the mission accomplished.

As intelligence and law enforcement personnel operating in environments other than our normal, we had to be more emotionally and cerebrally aware of the people we worked with – whether it was the local Middle Eastern security service we were collaborating with to take down a terrorist cell; or the local police in California as we tried to infiltrate a Russian Organized

Crime organization. We had to be aware of their mindset, their motivations and their lifestyles so that we could understand them, and their knowledge, and achieve our organizational objectives.

Emotional awareness sounds like a soft-skill and it is. We must be aware of our own emotions and the emotional states of those around us. Both at work and at home, these are critical skills. They help us remain in a state of reality – making good decisions because we have accurate information about the conditions under which they are being made. Emotional awareness is a big part of emotional intelligence, which is your ability to understand your current emotional state (happy, sad, depressed, excited), your ability to make decisions about it, and your ability to improve that state and others' as well. Emotional intelligence also allows an individual to anticipate what feelings they will have in the future based on events that may take place.

Emotional awareness allows you to move through your day, adjusting to difficulties as they come up. You are able to communicate to your loved ones more clearly about what you think about your child's performance in school, an issue in the neighborhood or an intimate issue with your spouse. Not only are you able to communicate more clearly to others, but you will better understand those who are trying to tell you how they are feeling.

It's critical to understand when you need to tell someone that they have crossed a line in how they are treating you. Your personal boundaries must be set. If you don't understand where yours are, it's likely people will intrude on those boundaries regularly, making you unhappy and leading you to bad decisions and places you do not want to go in your life.

People need emotional awareness in order to better understand what makes them mad, happy, sad, depressed. They can then make decisions to self-manage through the adversity presented to them, the good times and the bad times. This helps them level set their reality. This is key to mental and emotional health as poor management of emotions can lead to anxiety, depression, addictive behaviors, disassociation, and eating disorders.

If we are emotionally aware of ourselves and our spouses, we have a much higher likelihood of clear communication with our families. They will understand us better and they will learn from us. Our spouses are frequently perceived as our partners in life. We need them to navigate the challenges of modern life, the excess stimuli, the bad actors, the noise, and the distractions from what we are trying to achieve. As we work with our partner on a critical item – raising the children or navigating our careers, we must understand how they are feeling. Different aspects include: where we live, the commutes we have to endure, what schools they kids will attend, how they are performing, any challenges they may be feeling (e.g., bullying or being bullied, peer pressure, embarrassment, sex, drugs, and moving through adolescence.) As spouses, we need to be on the same sheet emotionally. If we are constantly out of sync, then we can expect bad communication, conflict, missteps, confusion and additional opportunities for the Jackal to take advantage.

It is critical to be aware of your reality, your family's context and conditions in which they are living and reacting.

If you can achieve REAL Awareness, a level of emotional awareness and situational awareness where your mind and body are maturely adjusting to the conditions around you, this is a great step towards being prepared for the Jackal.

If you can manage your REAL Awareness, you can move more safely towards your 1 Goal, to survive and thrive.

Apply the Color Codes of Awareness to your personal, family, and business environment. Do NOT operate in the white.

With your family, increase your awareness of neighborhood skills and abilities.

In the business, build a dashboard of stoplight charts that address the critical pieces of information to which you should be paying regular attention.

Emotional awareness is important to family and business relationships. It increases overall awareness and the ability to anticipate. Those who don't exercise it create chaos and are far less attuned to those around them and their needs.

120

16

REAL MINDSET

Mindset plays a critical role in your psychological and biophysical response to fear and danger. Do you have a positive outlook on life, a constructive mindset? In your business, do you exercise a growth mindset? When you travel the world and enter new crime and health environments, what kind of mindset do you employ then? I propose that you cannot carry with you the same mindset and expect the Jackals to stay away. The Jackals are different in different cultures, different cities and different neighborhoods.

As you mature in your life, take a spouse, have children and evolve in your prosperity and place in society, you have to maintain your mindset and it needs to be a **REAL Mindset.**

In the FBI we are taught that a survival mindset is key to surviving a critical incident that involves violence, medical emergencies, or severe emotional distress. This can be experienced as a trained special agent, a bystander who witnesses the event, a first responder who arrives on the scene, or as a victim. Any significant emotional event has a number of victims, and they are from all of the above groups. Once in the FBI, many of us had the privilege to share those training experiences with other law enforcement and community groups.

In our personal and business lives, we are encouraged to have a growth mindset, that we are always progressing, learning, maturing and improving ourselves and our businesses based on an open-minded perspective of life. That doesn't mean that people are unaware of negative influences, adversity, or setbacks. That's why you are reading this book. It just means that we are open and optimistic about understanding the inputs we are receiving and using those inputs in a constructive, growth mode to become better people, citizens, parents, or spouses.

But when the Jackal arrives, it is imperative that we are not sitting back in a negative mindset. We cannot be catastrophizing the scenarios at first blush, or saying out loud, "We are really going to screw this up. I know it." That is a recipe for failure. You need to avoid the negative energy, and falling into thinking traps that can take over our thinking under stress.

How do you think a SWAT operator or EMT would perform if their mindset was NOT already set on success? They have to be ready to take down the criminal behind that barricaded door, or stop that catastrophic bleeding wound right away by using their training and their operational mindset. They would not do well, and would not have made it through their selection, assessment, and training if they did NOT have a positive, survival mindset. It comes with the territory.

According to former FBI SWAT Sniper Stacey Mitry, it's important to have an empowered mindset. This is good for child development, professional development, personal security and for any challenge that is placed in our way of achieving our goals.

> Joe Buck questioned Max Scherzer, professional baseball player for the Washington Nationals, on how he was handling this abbreviated and modified 2020 baseball season:
>
> Q: How do you help the young players get ready for this shortened season, the stresses of COVID-19 and the lack of routine. They need to be ready and be fit without going

overboard in their workouts, or not being ready enough? Or being able to handle a positive test result for the illness.

Max: "I don't have a formula. We just have to take it in stride and keep moving forward. There is always going to be something every day, scheduling, or something. (His teammate Juan Soto had just tested positive for COVID-19.) "You just have to keep a smile on your face . . . be ready to go."

Not only is it critical for you to have the right mindset but it's also critical that your teammates and your family members have the same mindset. Let's take a hostage rescue for example, or trying to stop an active shooter in a school. How important would it be for you to understand your partner as you moved through that environment? The communication, the teamwork and the essential understanding of what your partner is going to do next is critical in a given scenario. Will they watch your back? What if you get injured?

You have to be prepared to act in tandem, in sync, or as a unit. The mindset must be set ahead of time and trained. What will happen as we enter the next classroom? What's behind that closed door? What will my partner do when he enters the room? Will he go left, right? Will he take the hard corner or hesitate in the doorway? If you know your partner well, if you have trained with each other, you understand them and you can make better decisions.

But all of that goes out the window once someone is shot if the mindset isn't there. The team could fragment and the cohesion is stressed. That's why special teams go through such rigorous examination and assessment to see if they have what it takes. The assessment determines if they bring to the team the right mindset, perhaps through military training in a former life. College athletics and former law enforcement training typically provide individuals with an edge going into selection for these teams. That is because they have winning, survival, growth mindsets that allow them to deal with losing, setbacks on and off the court, expending the energy to improve during practice and learning from mistakes.

Here are 10 things to help you move to a empowered, growth mindset, a REAL mindset. Tip of the hat to Stacey Mitry, former FBI Agent and SWAT Sniper, for some of these.

1. **Embrace Challenges, Seek Them Out**
   Failures are not your limits; you aren't a fixed object in time and space. You can change, you can evolve. Take on new challenges. Stretch your envelope of opportunity.

2. **View Growth and Life As A Process**
   Life is a process of developing. We are always learning and you can internalize the challenges as a necessary step in growth. It's not always about the end goal, but it might require you to temporarily focus on a near term goal that is critical to getting you to where you want to be. Think about it as a mountain climbing trip. It's a process. Decide to climb the mountain. Set a plan and a budget. Hire the guides. Buy the plane tickets. Get to the base. Start the climb. Make it to the first campsite. Get through the weather. Acclimate to the altitude. Achieve the next leg, arriving at your next bivouac. Achieving each milestone, and dealing with the challenges there; but not losing sight of the long-term goal.

3. **Be A Manifestation Farmer**
   Plant the seeds for ambitions and personal passions. Take a class for a new skill. Stretch your legs on a new topic. Don't keep going back to the old, safe concepts for a repeat performance. What works for you, won't work for others, but what's new for you in a class, or practical exercise, might bring you greater resilience opportunities.

4. **Accept That Everyone Stumbles**

No one is perfect. And no decision will be perfect. You must accept this. You aren't the first one addressing these issues, and you won't be the last. Keep going. Get enough information to make a good decision, and do not worry about what might have happened if you had more. You don't. Make the call. Deal with the outcome. Drive on.

5. **Own Your Space**

Fill the space around you with confidence. Head high, shoulders back, eye contact. You got this. Start small, feel the power, keep flourishing.

6. **Preparation Matters**

Stacy saw the pull-up requirement for the FBI SWAT team as daunting, especially when you added the 25-pound Kevlar vest. She trained hard and she was ready. When she succeeded, she recounted that she was prepared: mind, body and soul, for that moment. She crushed it.

7. **Situational Awareness**

Understand and acknowledge the good and bad around you. Educate yourself and your family on personal safety. Knowledge over fear builds empowerment. Know what's going on around you so that you can see them BEFORE they happen.

8. **Have a Backup Crew**

This empowers you to, as I like to say, "Dare to Fail." If you know you have supportive relationships, you can reach farther, try harder, with less fear of failure.

9. **Body Positivity**

For men and women. No myths, no magazines, no comparisons. Embrace what you have and strive to make it what you want. Your strength is within you.

Stacy became a FBI SWAT Sniper at 5'4" and 115 pounds. Embrace the mindset, train, achieve. Own it.

10. Make Resilience a Life Choice
Choice is a powerful thing. Choose to survive and thrive.

To fail and keep going is what being human is all about. Dare to fail, live to win. When we take failure as a given, as part of life – we give ourselves permission to try and try again without embarrassment; without shame. You are living your life.

Use the REAL Mindset to see the world positively, as achievable - and as recoverable when things go wrong. The world offers unlimited possibilities.

Yes, it can be daunting – but in the end, YOU can make your path – and YOU will survive and thrive.

17

REAL FITNESS

REAL Fitness is about ensuring your mental, emotional, and physical condition is healthy. You should have a high level of self-acceptance and esteem. You need to stay educated and informed. This level of REAL Fitness is also tied to awareness as you can understand and manage your emotions when you are fit. All of these have specific impacts on your ability to make good decisions and to react well to life's misfortunes. Of course, your level of physical fitness plays a specific role in reducing anxiety, increasing self-esteem and cardiovascular health. Diet and sleep are also critical in this category. Overall, each aspect depends on the other as one could be very physically fit, but be an emotional or mental basket case. The ability to run marathons or lift weights would have little bearing on your ability to deal with hardships.

Stress management is a key subset of REAL Fitness. If you cannot manage stress, you will not make good decisions during challenging times or under adverse conditions. Overall fitness can help you manage stress.

Mental fitness is about being aware of your social, financial, physical being. And then being mindful about all of it, eliminating negative thinking (which goes along with REAL

Mindset), and being constructive instead of being destructive. Being mindful can be as simple as a 20-minute walk in nature or a 10-minute meditation in a quiet room at work. Being aware of your breath, your heartbeat, reducing your stress and anxiety level and being present. Clearing our minds of all the noise, and focusing on the good, positive things is helpful. We can leave the sarcasm and negative energy of your officemate behind and focus on the positive outcomes of the day.

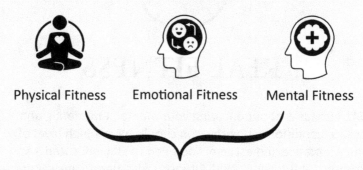

Physical Fitness   Emotional Fitness   Mental Fitness

High Level of Self-Acceptance and Esteem

Many specialists in the area of mindfulness believe we are what we think. That what we believe and say brings about the negative energies and actions of others. We should visualize, like professional athletes, the correct, positive outcome that we desire and NOT focus on what could be a negative outcome. This is another thinking trap.

Dr. Rick Hanson, a clinical psychologist and author of the 2018 book, *Resilient*, shared how we can build our resilience when adversity strikes. Hanson, a senior fellow at the Greater Good Science Center at the University of California, Berkeley, suggests that you calm and center yourself.

The people who survive significant emotional events are the people who are calm and centered and do not panic. Hanson opines that carving out just a few minutes each day to just sit there calmly and stare into space can do wonders for your well-being. Some people will meditate or pray, or exercise, or take the dog out for a walk. In short, being able to calm your body is absolutely fundamental to being resilient.

We need to know that it is our thoughts that cause emotions, not the things around us that make us angry. It is how we think about that other driver that incurs the road rage when we are cut off-it's not that you have a personal relationship with that stranger and therefore want to retaliate. It's not that his car was better than yours and you are angry with the car. It's not the things, but your thoughts about what just happened that cause you to lose control.

This brings us to emotional fitness, which is tied to emotional awareness that we spoke of earlier in this book. Are your emotions valid? Do you have a good reason to be sad? If your spouse is feeling sad, you can discuss this topic as adults to better understand their emotions.

Mental, emotional and physical REAL fitness must be maintained.

Source: Red Five

You can change your inner voice to be more positive. You can understand your emotions, validate them, and then learn from them by changing your behavior. This can be worked on with your spouse, your children and your parents. Be on the lookout for negative words and phrases and be more self-aware about your tone and how you talk to people.

You can practice good emotional fitness by being mindful and by getting into a routine that allows you to be self-aware of your thoughts. You can change your thinking to a more positive tone, a more constructive set of habits in your day. And lastly, you can make a difference with your family, your friends, your co-workers and business partners if you can be more emotionally fit. Reduce the drama and enjoy less self-induced stress from your own emotions.

Physical fitness is not necessarily about the weights you can lift and the miles you run each day. Mood is dramatically affected by the level of fitness and how often you engage in sport or a physical activity. The brain produces different chemicals when your body is put into a state of exertion, particularly competitive sports that utilize parts of your brain that are not in your daily routine for work. You hear about elite athletes getting into the zone.

That zone is a combination of chemicals and improved concentration and focus. If you are focused on the goal of winning the race, climbing the rock face, or getting through the next turn at a high speed, you are NOT thinking about whether or not you submitted that expense report last Friday. You are NOT thinking about closing that next real estate deal next week. Your thinking is sharpened and you are applying good judgment to the activity at hand. In motorcycling, you are visualizing the bike approaching the curve, braking at the right times, leaning the bike correctly, and accelerating out of the curve at the right time and place. At that moment, you are NOT trying to figure out what you will be texting your spouse at the next stop for gas.

Increased physical exertion will improve your sleep, as long as it's done at a time that makes sense in your normal cycle. I typically sleep much better when I'm regularly exercising, and finding time to get outside in the sunshine. Your weight and cardiopulmonary health will improve as your exercise regimen becomes more regular.

Mentally, we experience improvements in our self-confidence, and we may be more successful in our romantic efforts, our business leadership, and in how we interact with our children and spouses when we regularly exert ourselves in a positive and constructive fashion. We must stay mobile as we age. Immobility and lack of flexibility are killers in our modern world. Get off your ass and move. Do not sit idly by while the world passes you by.

Setting an example for your children, your spouse, or co-workers is an excellent by-product of a good physical fitness program. Children will benefit from getting into a routine of activity, even if it is merely going for walks or playing in the backyard, better there than inside staring at a screen in a sedentary state. It's better for their muscles, their development, their eyesight and their social skills to get them out and living their lives actively.

REAL Fitness isn't about the miles you run or the weights you lift. You need energy, flexibility, endurance. It is physical, mental, and emotional.

This applies to your family's operational flexibility, constructive outlook, and positive well-being. The more fit you, your family, and your business are – the better prepared you will be to manage stress.

In business, pay attention to your cash flow, debt ratio, hiring, and monitor accounts payable compared to accounts receivable. Try to offer diverse services and products, and optimize your supply chain.

What is your fitness plan?

REAL SKILLS

REAL Skills include those activities you know that can help you survive and thrive. These skills are not alien to many of you – these are skills you learned in school, at Boy or Girl Scouts, perhaps in a church youth group, summer camp, or in a club. First aid, automotive mechanics, basic computer skills, land navigation, self-defense, shelter construction, living in the outdoors, making a fire and finding food are all basic skills. As you progress and improve, you can add home defense, rural operations, international travel, and urban survival skills to your portfolio.

We believe in stress inoculation; immersing our participants in artificially stressful environments that work towards adding a specific skill (or skills) so that individuals can be tested under the right conditions with realistic stressors. These are significant stressors that raise the level of fear and adrenaline, and do so in a realistic environment – sometimes with role players, always with intensity. These environments ideally include an assault on all the senses – feel, smell, hearing, touch, and visual stimuli. Different people will react differently. We all know what it is like to be in a car when one person vomits – it can sometimes cause a chain reaction. Or perhaps we arrive at a campground to find someone with a bad injury and a lot of blood – do you faint at the sight of blood?

The active shooter scenario that tragically occurred at Columbine High School in Columbine, Colorado in April 1999 was an assault on the senses when law enforcement arrived on the scene. There were, of course, screaming children. But what most people don't realize is that the school sprinkler system was going off because of the improvised bombs that the killers set off, the fire alarms were blaring and the school was visually a war zone with bodies, backpacks, water and blood. The smell of cordite from firearms and smoke from the bombs was prevalent. The floor felt slippery from the water, and the blood. Their vision as they tried to find the killers was impaired by the sprinklers and smoke.

While many of the officers had been through their basic academy training-and some were SWAT certified-nothing, no amount of realistic training was able to prepare them for what they were seeing. Some who had served in the Persian Gulf War in the early nineties, or had been in Bosnia with the U.S. Military had some experience, but this was truly overwhelming.

REAL Training should be done in a constructive environment, preferably outside the classroom in a realistic condition – those must still be controlled and safe. When the old person must be stripped away and replaced with the warrior, the new, stronger version of oneself, then screaming and breaking down of the individual makes sense. This would be much like Boot Camp for the military. Once the adult has committed to adding skills, it's now about learning as professional adults. And yes, the adult learner will get out of it as much as they put into it.

Perhaps we provide the fundamental skills needed to protect your residence. We run participants through scenario after scenario with a real intruder, in the dark, with different layouts to present those learners real decisions to make under stress. The participants get to learn from hearing, watching, doing and receiving constructive feedback. When the home alarm goes off . . . do you turn on the lights or not? Is that a friend or foe?

Do you escape or harden your position? Do you apply lethal force with a firearm, or not?

What about wilderness medicine? You are on a day hike with your family just outside of San Francisco in Napa Valley. Your family finds itself in a position without cell service when your son slips off the trail and falls down a short ravine but incurs a bad break in a leg bone. Do you have the most basic of wilderness skills to get to him, stabilize him, and also to simultaneously find a way to get help?

We should talk about what it would take to escape from an urban area under duress after a major terror attack. If a dirty bomb were to make staying in your neighborhood dangerous and your family had to evacuate in an urban environment, do you have the skills needed to safely move out of the area? We spoke earlier of shelter in place or evacuate. In this instance, staying means possibly exposing you and your family to dangerous radiation. There is an evacuation order and the winds are not blowing in your favor. Do you have the urban skills to navigate out of a major city?

When an obstacle presents itself, you have to communicate.

Source: Red Five

We can add one more scenario with some level of likelihood. That is of international travel while on a work assignment or on a vacation. Picture yourself downtown for dinner in a country that is friendly but completely foreign in culture and language. You hear a large noise, possibly an explosion, and people begin running. You run into the street to see what's happened only to find yourself flat on your back. Stunned, you notice you are bleeding from your torso. Some questions that come out of this scenario include: Who are you traveling with? Can you communicate to get help? You find yourself being carried to a clinic by strangers. What is your blood type? Is it safe to receive blood transfusion in this country? How do you pay for services when they don't accept U.S. currency or credit cards?

Some skills come in the form of self-help, post-traumatic stress, or post-incident support for officers, victims, and military members and their family. Some of those skills can be applied in a way that helps identify a risk, such as with suicide prevention. The U.S. Army has spent large amounts of resources to address resiliency among its soldiers and also helps address issues for all military members through its resiliency programs.

 U.S. Army Resiliency Training: How to Avoid Catastrophic Thinking

Five steps to take when dealing with catastrophic thoughts

- Step 1: Describe the activating event
- Step 2: Capture worst case thoughts
- Step 3: Generate best case thoughts
- Step 4: Identify most likely outcomes
- Step 5: Develop a plan for dealing with most likely outcomes

This is best articulated in the U.S. Army's Suicide Prevention Program. They endeavor to prevent suicide among military members and their families. Everyone can help prevent suicide. Know how to recognize common risk factors including chronic pain; feelings of guilt, anger, or shame; exposure to trauma; a sense of hopelessness; relationship problems; and post-traumatic stress disorder. If you are experiencing any of these behaviors or notice them in friends and family who have served in the military, encourage them to seek help right away.

All of these have some similarities. They all have elements of awareness, contingency planning, medical skills and information, self and home defense, safe mobility, and communication.

Regardless of culture or conditions, acquiring REAL Skills is critical.

Source: Red Five

Training is available. But know that not all training is considered equal. For example, concealed carry is not training – it typically is firearm safety, storage, and legal advice on the basic laws surrounding firearms in your jurisdiction. You have met the compliance standard. Congratulations. Now what happens when the front door to your house is kicked in and your weapon is locked in a safe, unloaded, and secured with a trigger lock? You're not really operational.

When the neighbor has a heart attack and your CPR skills come in handy, that's good. Hopefully you can save their life – that's an applicable, real skill. Don't get me wrong, some basic training is good and applicable. Hopefully all you'll need is the basics.

The Jackal doesn't just test your skills, he tests you. As you travel the world, and find yourself in new environments, know that things change.

Conditions are different when your adversaries don't care about the basic value of human life, and will kill you for your case of bottled water. Or, you haven't planned well enough to save yourself from a lack of preparedness – not enough water and no map to get you home on that day hike two miles outside of town.

Assumptions can kill us. And yes, the Jackal will mock you for your lack of REAL readiness. He'll laugh and then he'll make life miserable.

How ready are you? Everyone can learn new skills and it's important to know your skill gaps and work to fill them with REAL skills.

Got skills? If not – go get them.

19

REAL RELATIONSHIPS

Human beings need to be around other human beings. We are social animals ourselves. We prefer to be in a tribe in most instances, moving in a societal group with a common cause. We find commonalities, choose our tribe or our society, perhaps by culture, language, needs, or geography. We know that we can benefit from being in a society that has diversity in skill sets, a variety of martial, vocational and professional skills that make our communities and our neighborhoods more resilient.

Relationships are critical before, during, and after misfortunes, disasters, illnesses, and challenges. Relationships have proven critical after our warriors come home from the war zone, experiencing injuries, PTSD, family challenges, etc. Our friends at the Warrior Canine Connection in Maryland put in countless hours to train and place dogs into the families of veterans to help them with their rehabilitation and return to civilian life.

During the Tsunami of 2004, it was found that relationships were critical in the recovery effort. Community relationships were particularly helpful in the recovery of agricultural aspects, and getting food and income moving again in the rural areas. They worked together with the non-government organizations to do land rehabilitation, cultivation, and application for resources and grants to help with recovery. In many instances, government or NGO support was not present or available, and it was friends and families that came to the aid of farmers by helping with cultivation, micro and family loans, and pure labor to help people get back on their feet.

> **"**
>
> Children who do well in the face of serious hardship typically have a biological resistance to adversity and strong relationships with the important adults in their family and community. Resilience is the result of a combination of protective factors. Neither individual characteristics nor social environments alone are likely to ensure positive outcomes for children who experience prolonged periods of toxic stress. It is the interaction between biology and environment that builds a child's ability to cope with adversity and overcome threats to healthy development.
> – Harvard University's Center on the Developing Child
>
> **"**

We all have parents and that is our first relationship. Most are healthy, some are not. We can learn from those who aren't, and we must remember that no one is perfect. Ideally our parents and grandparents, perhaps aunts and uncles, are supportive. They help to raise us as children and provide advice and mentoring when life presents us with new challenges – that first loss on the football field; how to deal with dating; the first job; or, perhaps leaving your home town for the military, college, or that first big job. We need support and our family should be providing that.

We find support in our friends, some of whom are fleeting and tied to a geography or a school; some of whom we are blessed to have for our whole lives. Like many adults, I can only name a handful of people who I still keep in touch with from my early school years. I am aware of friends from first grade, as I'm aware of losing friends from junior high, high school, and college from tragedies, cancer, terrorism, and crime. What we are looking for are supportive friends who are there for you when you need them. 99 percent of the time, Facebook friends will not count.

Persons undergoing health challenges, such as life-changing surgeries, or cancer, find that relationships are important before, during, and after treatment. According to the Mayo Clinic, "Whether you encounter problems with your relationships (after cancer) often depends on the strength of the relationships beforehand. Relationships that were already strained tend to continue that way after cancer, sometimes completely falling apart. Strong relationships can become even stronger through the cancer experience."

REAL Relationships and communication will help you overcome the obstacle.

Source: Red Five

Communications, culture, shared experiences (good and bad) and the ability to relate to each other is essential to filling the data set needed to get through debilitating illnesses and to even help you make good decisions day-to-day. This is the data set from which we draw the ability to establish plans, understand the environment in which people find themselves and make critical decisions about what actions to take next. **We must build and nurture relationships that matter, and REAL Relationships come out of these connections.**

Beliefs and values can play a strong part in one's resiliency around adversity. Does the family have a strong moral base? Perhaps there is school contingent or supporters from the local church to help the parents and kids get through the challenges they face.

Youth groups provide an architecture within which teens can be themselves but in a more spiritual context. They can perhaps air their concerns with advisors who are not their parents, but can still receive guidance from an adult perspective. I enjoyed two different youth groups growing up and they both provided me valuable experiences. I traveled with both and experienced different cities and seasons. I was fortunate to have great advisors in both and found it to be a constructive outlet for those tough years as a high school kid.

Teachers and college professors can play a role in helping students find themselves, rule out fleeting academic or career interests and nail down how they should pursue a vocation or career. In high school, I loved the gritty nature of auto mechanics and learned a lot about being practical and pragmatic with mechanical things. However, I did learn a lot about people and respecting their skills, especially when I didn't share that expertise.

Athletics can also be a place where individuals can find constructive relationships among their coaches and teammates. Many college athletes go on to be highly productive adults because of the skills and discipline that they learned coming up through the various ranks in their preferred sport. And if they are fortunate enough to find themselves involved in college sports, it's a whole new level of commitment, support and competition.

Mass quarantines and stay-at-home orders have been ongoing now for months as COVID-19 ravages the planet. These scenarios have us staying at home, in lockdown in some instances, as we wait for the virus to slow down. These confined conditions stress the relationships we have, and they change over time. As polar explorers and astronauts have both experienced, things are exciting and different as the adrenaline kicks in and you have a new "mission" – to get to space, to explore the arctic. But, then over time, that newness wears off. You find yourself very isolated in a quarantine situation. Those around you grow weary of your jokes and everyone experiences cabin fever. However, like the astronauts, if you have strong relationships, you can adjust and modify your environment with those around you. If your relationships were already stressed and struggling before

COVID-19, then those relationships continue to struggle.

According to Stacey Mitry, former FBI Special Agent, SWAT Operator and Sniper, having an empowered mindset is key, but having a "Backup Crew" is essential to that. But don't rely on that Crew as a crutch. It's an empowering thing to have strong relationships so you can dare to fail.

Having strong relationships, whether at home or at work, will help you weather the storm of a shelter-in-place situation; a polar adventure; or a trip to space. Let's make sure we have what it takes to get through the next challenge that is presented to us.

REAL Relationships are critical. They are sounding boards. They provide the support structure and guidance needed to respond to and bounce back from adversity.

Peers, family, friends, spouses, and significant others all play critical roles in our resilience.

Relationships are hard, they need nurturing – but they are worth it.

RESILIENCY IS A CHOICE

Taking Back Your Life

Many of you have grown up in a secure environment, flush with technology, streaming videos, little reason to get outside, less reason to take risks and control your destiny. We have enjoyed a luxurious, first-world existence in the U.S. This has been a golden age for some, but troubling times have already found some of us.

The pandemic and the civil unrest that is upon humanity today is a tragic, terrible development – one that could have been avoided, one that required true nation-wide leadership.

It is not about the politics; it is about the choices that individuals have made that have a direct impact on the citizens and people living in the world.

The choice is yours. You have freewill.

We need to make better choices as leaders in government and in business, in family activities, and for ourselves and as fellow Americans.

We have a choice in how we live our lives.

Do you want to be resilient? Or do you want to roll over and submit to the Jackals that roam this planet? Do you want to survive and thrive?

Do you want to be strong for your family?

Do you want your business and employees to thrive and profit in today's dynamic world?

Keep the 5-3-1 System in Your Back Pocket

It's not enough to say "I want to be happy." You must apply the 5 pillars to work towards happiness. I'm not saying it's hard, and I'm not saying it's easy. I'm saying that you have to be deliberate about what you want.

The founders of the U.S. did not wake up one day and say they wanted to be free from British rule. They argued, they deliberated on what it meant, then they chose to be free. Then they spoke out, they fought, and they died to be free. It is a mindset, like deciding to be REAL and resilient.

"FREEWILL"

by Rush

There are those who think that life
Has nothing left to chance
With a host of holy horrors
To direct our aimless dance

A planet of play things
We dance on the strings
Of powers we cannot perceive
"The stars aren't aligned -
Or the gods are malign"
Blame is better to give than receive

You can choose a ready guide
In some celestial voice
If you choose not to decide
You still have made a choice
You can choose from phantom fears
And kindness that can kill
I will choose a path that's clear
I will choose free will

Songwriters: Geddy Lee, Alex Lifeson, Neil Peart

Some can find happiness and success in other things that keep them busy, social media, pointless material things, and wasting time worrying about the future. Some can put their head in the sand, forego their power of choice and just let things happen as they may. Many believe that is an acceptable path forward. Some find a middle ground, that fate will take them wherever they need to be. Be active, not passive - but I add that your freewill and your power of choice is key.

You can choose to be resilient, ready, and prepared – to help yourself.

You can choose to exercise your freewill, choose to contribute, choose to cast your vote, choose to participate.

Choose resiliency. Choose to be REAL.

EPILOGUE

The world is not a safe place and change is constant. Be resilient.

Surviving and thriving is essential.

We are on this planet for a reason(s). Your reasons are different from others. There is a singular force, a supreme being, a God for each of us, who plays a role in how things play out. But I believe firmly that we have been empowered with freewill to play out our role, to be the best version of ourselves. And, that this all-powerful, all-knowing entity has a plan for us- has a hand in how it goes- but, allows us to make our own decisions.

There are bad people out there, and bad things that happen to us all. Each of us experiences adversity, some version of the Jackal taps us on the shoulder, knocks on the door of our family home, or arrives at our place of business. Evil is out there and it has many shapes and manifests itself in illness, natural disasters, bad business, violent weather, man-made criminal intent and malicious group-think in the form of terrorism and worse. You have to be ready for the Jackals.

If you want to live life to your fullest potential, see things, do things, be prosperous, healthy, and help living things, then you will need to survive and thrive. You need to achieve the one goal outlined in the REAL program. You can make things better.

As discussed, we have focused on **the 3 units . . . we** know the Jackals attack all three, and we know that to survive in a society, all three are critical to a successful life. The individual, the family and the business flows from the success. Do not neglect one for the other. Choose to live a life of resiliency – enhance your awareness, apply the mindset, get fit, build your skills, nurture your relationships.

Do not neglect the family readiness because you aren't married. Do not turn away from family and close friends because they may be your only family where you live today. Be open minded to the concept, and apply those readiness concepts to those you love, respect and treasure.

Do not ignore preparedness because you don't own your own business. You have a livelihood and you have a workplace – incorporate the preparedness pillars into your workplace. Find a champion in your place of employment and make things better. If you own your business, know that you have the most work ahead of you – you have a great responsibility to your employees, and you have the power, the authority, and the means to make your business better prepared today.

The 5 pillars of REAL Resilience should be applied across all three units – individual, family, and business. Recognize the differences in the pillars across the units, and don't be so rigid as to ignore the flexibility this system allows. Incorporate what makes sense, be smart about your budget for your training, your supplies, and your mindset. Don't fake it. Be accountable. **Be REAL.**

This book puts forth a reasonable, responsible, national-security minded approach to achieving resilience that is based on the individual, expanded upon for families, and modified to inform businesses in today's uncertain world. This isn't a radical movement; this isn't a militant approach.

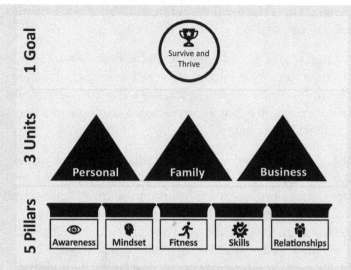

REAL Awareness – Be aware of yourself, others, and the conditions around you. Seek good information, and base your decisions on reality.

REAL Mindset – Have a positive, growth, survival mindset. Avoid the thinking traps and catastrophic, negative thinking.

REAL Fitness – Maintain positive emotional awareness, optimize your well-being, and energize your life with physical and mental fitness exercises that are based in mobility, flexibility, strength, and mindfulness.

REAL Skills – You need them, they have likely been neglected. Be sure to be able to defend yourself, your family, and your business – while at home, while working, and while in transit and during travel. These are achievable, learnable skills. Know your limitations, build on what you have, try new things that can make you better.

REAL Relationships – We all need support, whether from a friend, a parent, a peer, or a mentor. Seek out positive, constructive relationships in family, community, industry, and country. Go to those relationships when you need personal help, a sounding board for business, a sanity check on family, and advice about being resilient.

You now have the 5-3-1 System...

This book outlines a simple system, and sets forth the concepts that can be followed to be more resilient as a person, more ready as a family, and better prepared in your business and livelihood.

I challenge you to be resilient. To choose to live a life where you will survive and thrive.

I challenge you to be responsible for your family. Take care of them, make them more ready for the uncertain times, so that they can enjoy the easy times with the luxury of living in the moment.

I challenge you to ensure your livelihood and your business are prepared. With preparedness will come peace of mind, less distraction, better sleep and a result of those things will be profit, prosperity, affluence and fulfillment.

Resilience is a national security issue. With these REAL concepts adopted by like-minded citizens, I believe our country is more secure. It starts with you, the individual and relies upon the three units and the five pillars.

REAL resilience comes from a deliberate effort, a personal choice.

Use the freewill you have as a free individual. Make the choices.

Each morning, choose to be ready for anything. Don't fake it.
Be REAL.

Choose to be prepared.

Choose to be ready.

Choose to be resilient.

CPSIA information can be obtained
at www.ICGtesting.com
Printed in the USA
BVHW072247201020
591433BV00007B/11/J